The Institute of Chartered Accountants in England and Wales

PRINCIPLES OF TAXATION

For exams in 2018

Question Bank

www.icaew.com

ICAEW

Principles of Taxation
The Institute of Chartered Accountants in England and Wales

ISBN: 978-1-78363-885-7

Previous ISBN: 978-1-78363-461-3

First edition 2007
Twelfth edition 2017

British Library Cataloguing-in-Publication Data
A catalogue record for this book is available from the British Library

Originally printed in the United Kingdom on paper obtained from traceable,
sustainable sources.

Contents

The following questions are exam standard. Unless told otherwise, these questions are the style, content and format that you can expect in your exam.

Exam

This assessment consists of 42 questions in total. There will be 40 objective-test questions (80% of the marks) which will be of the following four types:

- Multiple choice – select 1 from 4 options A, B, C or D (Chapter 2 Q1)

- Multi-part multiple choice – select 1 from 2 or 3 options, for 2 or more question parts (see Chapter 2 Q2)

- Multiple response – select 2 or 3 responses from 4 or more options (Chapter 1 Q6)

- Numeric entry – rounded to the nearest pound (£)
  (Chapter 3 Q2)

There will be two scenario-based questions (20% of the marks) which will each cover a single syllabus area: income tax and NIC, and corporation tax.

The tax tables are provided on-screen in the assessment.

The assessment is 1.5 hours long and at least 55 marks are required to pass this assessment.

Our website has the latest information, guidance and exclusive resources to help you prepare for this assessment. Find everything you need, from exam webinars, sample assessments, errata sheets and the syllabus to advice from the examiners at icaew.com/exams if you're studying the ACA and icaew.com/cfabstudents if you're studying ICAEW CFAB.

Question Bank

Chapter 1: Ethics

1   Which of the following is **not** a fundamental principle of the IESBA Code of Ethics?

   A   Professional behaviour
   B   Professional intellect
   C   Integrity
   D   Objectivity
   E   Confidentiality   LO 1g

2   Professional accountants must be straightforward and honest in all professional and business relationships.

Select which of the following options correctly identifies this fundamental principle of the IESBA Code of Ethics.

   A   Professional behaviour
   B   Integrity

A professional accountant must comply with relevant laws and regulations and avoid any action that discredits the profession.

Select which of the following options correctly identifies this fundamental principle of the IESBA Code of Ethics.

   C   Professional behaviour
   D   Integrity
   E   Professional competence and due care   LO 1g

3   Sandra, a Chartered Accountant, is completing the corporation tax computation for a client company. She realises that the client company's sales director, Heather, is a close family friend. Heather asks Sandra whether she has seen any information from the Financial Director about any planned bonuses.

Which **two** of the fundamental principles of the IESBA Code of Ethics may be under threat here?

   A   Objectivity
   B   Integrity
   C   Professional behaviour
   D   Confidentiality   LO 1g

4   Richard, a Chartered Accountant who works as a sole trader, is aware that he must adhere to the IESBA fundamental principle of confidentiality in respect of information he acquires in the course of his work.

Which of the following describes a situation where Richard does **not** have to keep such information confidential?

   A   When he suspects a client of money laundering
   B   When his firm no longer acts for the client
   C   When his firm has not yet been engaged by a prospective client
   D   When talking to a close friend in a social environment   LO 1g

5   William, a Chartered Accountant, is being threatened by his client, James. James is threatening to harm William's family if William refuses to launder money for him.

Which of the following options correctly identifies the type of threat William is experiencing according to the IESBA Code of Ethics?

A   Self-interest threat
B   Self-review threat
C   Advocacy threat
D   Familiarity threat
E   Intimidation threat   LO 1g

6   Roger is a Chartered Accountant and is married to Jennifer, who is also his client. Jennifer runs several businesses on behalf of her father. Roger knows that Jennifer comes from a wealthy criminal family. However, Roger has never queried the funding of Jennifer's businesses as he trusts her implicitly.

Which **two** of the following options are threats Roger is experiencing according to the IESBA Code of Ethics?

A   Self-interest threat
B   Self-review threat
C   Advocacy threat
D   Familiarity threat
E   Intimidation threat   LO 1g

7   Florence, a Chartered Accountant, knows that a client, Freddy, has financed his business using the proceeds of his criminal activities for a number of years. Florence has not reported this and has instead accepted substantial payments from Freddy which are 10 times her normal fee for comparable work.

Which **two** of the following statements are correct?

A   Freddy is laundering money through his business and as Florence is aware of this she is required to disclose it to the proper authorities.

B   Florence should discuss her decision to go to the authorities with Freddy.

C   Florence may be guilty of money-laundering offences as she has assisted Freddy in concealing the proceeds of crime.

D   Florence was justified in increasing her fee for such risky work.   LO 1h

8   Iqmal is a Chartered Accountant who has just become suspicious that a client is engaged in money laundering.

Iqmal should report this to the firm's Money Laundering Reporting Officer

A   once there is sufficient proof of money laundering
B   now

Any Suspicious Activity Report would be made by

C   Iqmal
D   the firm's Money Laundering Reporting Officer   LO 1h

9   Select which of the following would be offences under UK anti-money laundering legislation:

   (1) An accountant alerting a money launderer that a report has been made to the NCA.
   (2) An accountant failing to report knowledge of a client's money-laundering activities.
   (3) A taxpayer underpaying tax as the result of a deliberate omission from their tax return.
   (4) A taxpayer underpaying tax as the result of an innocent error from their tax return.
   (5) The act of tax avoidance.

   A   All of them
   B   (1) to (3) only
   C   (2) and (3) only
   D   (2), (3) and (5) only   LO 1h

---

10   Which of the following is **not** one of the factors for consideration given in the framework for ethical conflict resolution in the ICAEW Code?

   A   Ethical issues involved
   B   Alternative courses of action
   C   Timescale involved
   D   Relevant parties   LO 1g

---

11   Identify in the following scenarios whether the professional accountant is committing an offence under the anti-money laundering legislation.

   Steven accepts payment from a client in relation to work performed in preparing his personal tax return. The fee is a percentage of the reduction in the tax payable based on the previous year. Steven strongly suspects that the client has failed to disclose all sources of income. He later discovers this to be the case.

   A   Offence committed by Steven
   B   No offence committed by Steven

   Trevor suspected that a client of his has been receiving income through the operation of a criminal cartel. He reported this to his firm's Money Laundering Reporting Officer (MLRO), but has not heard anything else from the MLRO. Trevor later approaches the client to advise him of his suspicions and that the firm may have to report this to the authorities.

   C   Offence committed by Trevor
   D   No offence committed by Trevor   LO 1h

---

12   A threat to the fundamental principles may occur when a professional accountant promotes a particular opinion, compromising subsequent objectivity.

   This category of threat is known as

   A   self-interest threat
   B   self-review threat
   C   advocacy threat
   D   familiarity threat   LO 1g

13 A threat to fundamental principles may occur when a professional accountant has to re-evaluate a previous judgement that he or she made.

This category of threat is known as

A   self-interest threat
B   self-review threat
C   advocacy threat
D   familiarity threat

LO 1g

14 Lauren is unhappy with an explanation given to her by a client in relation to the current year's accounts. If she accepts the explanation and submits the accounts to HMRC she feels that this will compromise the principle of integrity.

Which of the following factors is she **not** required to consider in resolving the ethical conflict?

A   The facts that she has uncovered
B   The relationship that her firm has with the client
C   The client's internal procedures
D   Alternative courses of action

LO 1g

15 Which of the following statements is correct?

A   Tax evasion is illegal and tax avoidance is legal.
B   Both tax evasion and tax avoidance are legal.
C   Tax evasion is legal and tax avoidance is illegal.
D   Both tax avoidance and tax evasion are illegal.

LO 1h

16 Mr Blythe is tendering for some consultancy work. The same work has also been tendered for by Comp Partners, the accountancy firm which prepares Mr Blythe's tax returns.

The ethics partner at Comp Partners concludes that the threat from this conflict of interest cannot be acceptably reduced.

According to the ICAEW Code, which of the following would be an acceptable course of action for Comp Partners?

A   Inform Mr Blythe of the conflict and notify him that Comp Partners is ceasing to act for him
B   Inform Mr Blythe of the conflict and obtain his written consent to continue to act for him
C   Inform Mr Blythe of the conflict and continue to act for him
D   Continue to act for Mr Blythe and keep the conflict confidential

LO 1h

17 Toby is a sole trader.

Which of the following actions by Toby is **not** an example of tax evasion?

A   Claiming £2,000 of personal expenses through the business

B   Understating cash sales by £500

C   Deliberately postponing the sale of some shares from 5 April until 6 April so that he can use the following year's annual exempt amount to reduce his capital gains tax

D   Overestimating the value of some property donated to charity

LO 1h

Chapter 2: Introduction to taxation

1   Which of the following items is **never** a source of UK tax law?

    A   The annual Finance Act
    B   HMRC statements of practice
    C   Case law
    D   Statutory instruments   LO 1f

2   Pauline used to earn £20,000 and paid £3,000 in income tax per annum. She has recently received a substantial pay rise and now earns £50,000. Her revised income tax is £10,000.

What is the principle on which this tax system is based?

    A   Progressive taxation
    B   Regressive taxation

National insurance contributions is an example of

    C   direct taxation
    D   indirect taxation   LO 1b

3   One argument proposed in debates about taxation, is that the cost of collecting tax should be low in relation to the tax raised.

The principle behind this argument is the

    A   ability to pay principle
    B   efficiency principle

VAT is an example of

    C   direct taxation
    D   indirect taxation   LO 1b

4   A government is considering abolishing the current VAT rules on all food bought in supermarkets (but not any other shop) and replacing it with the following form of taxation. Each item bought in the supermarket will be subject to a levy of £0.75. In other words a person who purchases 10 items of any value will pay £7.50 in tax.

The principle behind the proposed system is the

    A   ability to pay principle
    B   value principle
    C   unit principle
    D   neutrality principle   LO 1b

5   Which of the following is a source of tax law?

    A   The Budget
    B   Statutory instruments
    C   HMRC extra-statutory concessions
    D   HMRC statements of practice   LO 1f

6   Diana is an individual who does not have a trade or business of any kind. Diana is an employee earning £30,000 per year and a shareholder in Firm Ltd. Diana has heard that the following taxes exist in the UK and is unsure which of them she pays personally:

(1)   Capital gains tax
(2)   Corporation tax
(3)   Income tax
(4)   National insurance contributions
(5)   Value added tax

Which of the following options correctly identifies which taxes Diana could or does suffer personally?

A   All of them
B   (1), (3) and (4) only
C   (1), (3), (4) and (5) only
D   (1), (2), (3) and (4) only   LO 1e

7   John and David operate a VAT-registered partnership, employing a large number of staff.

Which of the following options correctly identifies which taxes the partners are jointly and severally liable for?

(1)   Income tax on each partner's share of profits from the partnership
(2)   Income tax of employees deducted under the Pay As You Earn (PAYE) system
(3)   Employer and employee national insurance contributions payable in respect of their staff
(4)   Capital gains tax on each partner's share of partnership gains
(5)   VAT as a supplier of goods

A   All of them
B   (1), (2) and (3) only
C   (2), (3) and (5) only
D   (1), (2), (3) and (5) only   LO 1e

8   Which of the following are functions carried out by HMRC?

(1)   Collect and administer direct taxes
(2)   Collect and administer indirect taxes
(3)   Pay and administer child support payments
(4)   Collect repayments of student loans
(5)   Pay and administer the state pension

A   (1) and (2) only
B   (1), (2) and (3) only
C   (1), (2) and (4) only
D   (1), (2), (3) and (5) only   LO 1e

9   Which of the following options is correct regarding case law, as determined by tax cases in court?

A   Case law is purely for guidance when interpreting statutory law.
B   Case law applies for the 12 months following the date of the particular court case.
C   Case law can be superseded by further statutory legislation.
D   Case law sets a precedent meaning the law can never be changed.   LO 1f

10   Which of the following options correctly describes a statutory instrument?

A   Published by HMRC primarily for the guidance of its own staff
B   Sets out HMRC's interpretation of tax legislation
C   Provides a relaxation of the strict legal position of tax legislation
D   Tax legislation, commonly in the form of Regulations, containing detailed provisions   LO 1f

1   Patrick has net income for 2017/18 is £117,750.

    What is his personal allowance for 2017/18? £ ⬚

    You may enter your answer as a positive or negative number   LO 3b

---

2   In 2017/18, Mackenzie has taxable income (after deducting the personal allowance) of £25,565 (non-savings income) and £1,100 (savings income).

    What is Mackenzie's total income tax liability for 2017/18? £ ⬚   LO 3j

---

3   William, now aged 85, married Grainne, now aged 73, on 10 December 2005. In 2017/18 William received income from his pension of £7,000. For many years Grainne has run a small shop and her business has made adjusted trading profits of £18,000 for 2017/18. The couple have no other sources of income.

    The married couples allowance due to the couple for 2017/18 will initially be

    A   given to William
    B   given to Grainne
    C   shared between them equally

    The allowance due to the couple to give relief at 10% is

    D   £845
    E   £11,500
    F   £8,445   LO 3b

---

4   During 2017/18 Kael had taxable income (after deduction of the personal allowance) of £35,530 (non-savings income) and £6,200 (dividend income). Tax of £6,805 has been deducted from Kael's non-savings income. He also paid £720 as a Gift Aid donation to his son's school (a registered charity).

    What is Kael's income tax payable by self assessment for 2017/18?

    A   £917
    B   £2,542
    C   £1,097
    D   £7,722   LO 3j

---

5   In 2017/18, Paloma has taxable income (after deduction of the personal allowance) of £88,500 (all dividend income).

    What is Paloma's income tax liability for 2017/18?

    A   £23,575
    B   £20,388
    C   £20,013
    D   £18,763   LO 3j

6   On 20 May 2017 Charlie, aged 73 married Sarah, aged 83. In 2017/18 Charlie and Sarah had net income of £15,000 and £12,000 respectively.

How much married couple's allowance can Charlie claim as a tax reducer for 2017/18?

A   £844
B   £774
C   £387
D   £422   LO 3b

---

7   In 2017/18, Glenn has taxable income (after deducting the personal allowance) of £28,500 (non-savings income) and £5,300 (dividend income).

What is Glenn's total income tax liability for 2017/18? £ [   ]   LO 3j

---

8   In 2017/18 Mabel had taxable income (after deducting the personal allowance) of £39,000, all of which represented savings income. She paid £1,056 as a Gift Aid donation to the NSPCC (a registered charity).

What is Mabel's income tax liability for 2017/18? £ [   ]   LO 3j

---

9   During 2017/18 Jacob gave a cash donation of £2,000 to a registered charity. His only income is an annual salary of £50,000.

Identify how Jacob obtains tax relief for his gift.

He receives basic rate tax relief

A   at source by deduction from his salary under payroll giving
B   at source by paying net of basic rate income tax
C   by extending the basic rate band

He receives higher rate tax relief

D   at source by deduction from his salary under payroll giving
E   at source by paying net of basic rate income tax
F   by extending the basic rate band   LO 3j

---

10   Puneet's only source of income in 2017/18 is a salary of £102,730.

What is his personal allowance for 2017/18?

A   £11,500
B   £10,135
C   £8,770
D   £1,365   LO 3b

---

11   In 2017/18, Pierre had taxable income (after deducting the personal allowance) of £3,000 (non-savings income), £2,800 savings income and £1,500 dividend income.

What is his income tax liability for 2017/18?

A   £660
B   £760
C   £600
D   £960   LO 3j

12   Margaret is self-employed and has taxable trading profits (after deduction of the personal allowance) of £30,000 in 2017/18. During 2017/18 Margaret also received dividend income of £9,000.

How much of Margaret's dividend income is subject to tax at 32.5% in 2017/18?

A   £500
B   £5,500
C   £4,000
D   £9,000   LO 3j

13   Maalik is employed by Artichoke Ltd and has taxable income in 2017/18 of £20,000 (after deduction of the personal allowance). On 1 December 2017 Maalik paid £420 to a charity under the Gift Aid provisions.

In 2017/18 the Gift Aid payment will

A   increase Maalik's income tax liability
B   decrease Maalik's income tax liability
C   have no impact on Maalik's income tax liability
D   generate a refund of income tax payable to Maalik   LO 3j

14   In 2017/18, Bussola has taxable non-savings income (after deduction of the personal allowance) of £210. During 2017/18 she also received taxable savings income of £38,100.

What is Bussola's income tax liability for 2017/18? £ [   ]   LO 3j

15   Manav has taxable income (after deduction of the personal allowance) in 2017/18 of:

Non-savings income   £17,015
Savings income   £1,800

What is Manav's income tax liability for 2017/18? £ [   ]   LO 3j

16   Frederick works as an employee of Wood Ltd. Frederick's only source of income is employment income. Frederick's taxable income (after deduction of the personal allowance) for 2017/18 was £15,815. During 2017/18 Frederick paid £3,100 in income tax via PAYE.

What is Frederick's income tax payable under self-assessment for 2017/18? £ [   ]

                                                                                      LO 3j

17   Sidney and Bertha were married in February 2007. Sidney is now aged 69 and Bertha is now aged 85. For 2017/18 Sidney has net income of £6,788 and Bertha has net income of £13,456.

What is Sidney's married couple's allowance for 2017/18?

A   £0 – Allocated to Bertha
B   £11,500
C   £8,445
D   £3,220   LO 3b

18   Darcy is self employed and has trading profits assessable in 2017/18 of £198,000.

What is Darcy's personal allowance for 2017/18? £ [   ]

You may enter your answer as a positive or negative number   LO 3b

19 Dave has taxable income in 2017/18 of £133,000 (non-savings income), £27,600 (savings income) and £15,000 (dividend income).

What is Dave's income tax liability for 2017/18?

A £61,350
B £63,785
C £61,430
D £61,880

LO 3j

---

20 Diane is self employed and has trading profits assessable in 2017/18 of £118,000.

What is Diane's personal allowance for 2017/18? £ [   ]

You may enter your answer as a positive or negative number

LO 3b

---

21 Sandra has rental profits assessable in 2017/18 of £128,000.

What is Sandra's personal allowance for 2017/18? £ [   ]

You may enter your answer as a positive or negative number

LO 3b

---

22 Geoff had taxable income (after deduction of his personal allowance) of £14,450 of non-savings income in 2017/18. His wife, Jessica, had no income during 2017/18. Jessica made a marriage allowance election in 2017/18.

What is Geoff's income tax liability for 2017/18? £ [   ]

LO 3j

---

23 During 2017/18 Leanne was a higher rate taxpayer (net income of £80,000) but her husband Richard stayed at home to look after their children, and had no income in 2017/18. Both Leanne and Richard are aged 40.

Which of the following statements about the personal allowance is **true**?

A Leanne's personal allowance is reduced because her income exceeds the basic rate band.
B An election can be made to transfer all of Richard's personal allowance to Leanne.
C An election can be made to transfer £1,150 of Richard's personal allowance to Leanne.
D No election can be made to transfer any part of Richard's personal allowance to Leanne.

LO 3b

---

24 Sarah who was born in 1938, has net income in 2017/18 of £29,000. She married Arthur, who was born in 1931, in March 2010. Arthur has net income for 2017/18 of £15,000.

What is Sarah's married couple's allowance for 2017/18 on which 10% tax relief is given?

£ [   ]

LO 3b

---

25 Shelia who was born in 1936, has net income in 2017/18 of £39,300. She married Archie, who was born in 1932, in January 2007. Archie has net income for 2017/18 of £12,000.

What is Shelia's married couple's allowance for 2017/18 on which 10% tax relief is given?

£ [   ]

LO 3b

Chapter 4: Employment income

1   Emily is an employee of Door Ltd with a gross annual salary of £26,000. In addition Emily has taxable benefits worth £4,208. Emily underpaid her tax for 2016/17 by £246. Emily has agreed with HMRC that this underpayment will be collected via her PAYE code for 2017/18.

What is Emily's PAYE code for 2017/18?

A   606L
B   704L
C   729L
D   1150L   LO 2b

2   Mustafa is an employee of Window Ltd with a gross annual salary of £17,000. Mustafa underpaid his tax for 2016/17 by £840. Mustafa has agreed with HMRC that this underpayment will be collected via his PAYE code for 2017/18.

What is Mustafa's PAYE code for 2017/18?

A   730L
B   940L
C   1066L
D   1150L   LO 2b

3   Parminder is an employee of Sales Ltd with a gross annual salary of £50,000. Parminder also has taxable benefits worth £17,550 for 2017/18.

What is Parminder's PAYE code for 2017/18?

PAYE code [   ]   LO 2b

4   James earns £60,000 a year. He is entitled to a basic personal allowance. His employer provides him with a company car with a taxable benefit of £12,775.

What is James' PAYE code for 2017/18?

A   K126
B   K127
C   K128
D   127L   LO 2b

5   Jacob earns £15,000 a year. His employer provides him with taxable benefits of £4,560.

What is Jacob's PAYE code for 2017/18? [   ] L   LO 2b

6   Dana has total income of £50,000 each year. She has underpaid tax of £1,232 in 2016/17 which is recovered through her PAYE code in 2017/18.

What is Dana's PAYE code for 2017/18?

A   534L
B   842L
C   1026L
D   1150L   LO 2b

Chapter 5: Trading profits

1   Which **two** of the following statements indicate that a trade is being carried on?

   A   Amy has just sold a house that she bought three months ago. She has spent £40,000 to make the property more attractive to potential purchasers. Amy has not lived in this house.

   B   Ben has sold some shares that he has owned for 10 years for substantially more than the original cost.

   C   Caitlin, a student, has cash flow problems and sells a car that she bought three months ago.

   D   Dante has an interest in vintage cars. He has just sold a car that he has been renovating for the last six months. This is the seventh renovated car that he has sold in the last two years.

   LO 3d

2   Which **two** of the following are **not** badges of trade?

   A   The number of transactions
   B   Provision of own equipment
   C   Profit seeking motive
   D   Changes to the asset
   E   Correction of own work

   LO 3d

3   Penha has a hobby restoring antique furniture. He has just sold a restored antique table that he has owned for several years. He sold 10 items of restored furniture in 2017/18.

   Which **two** of the following badges indicate that Penha is carrying on a trade in relation to this disposal?

   A   The number of transactions
   B   Interval of time between purchase and sale
   C   Changes to the asset
   D   Correction of own work

   LO 3d

4   According to the badges of trade, HMRC would probably view the purchase of 1,000,000 toilet rolls by an individual as being carried out

   A   for personal use
   B   for their aesthetic value
   C   for long-term investment
   D   to be sold at a profit

   LO 3d

Chapter 6: Capital allowances

1   Nina began trading on 1 January 2017 and prepared accounts for the year ended 31 December 2017. On 1 August 2017 she purchased a photocopier for £2,300 and a car with emissions of 128g/km for £2,300. The photocopier and the car are both used for business purposes for 90% of the time.

The maximum capital allowances that Nina will receive in respect of the purchase of the photocopier in the year ended 31 December 2017 are

A   £2,300
B   £2,070
C   £373

The maximum capital allowances that Nina will receive in respect of the purchase of the car in the year ended 31 December 2017 are

D   £2,300
E   £414
F   £373

LO 3e

2   Aasia began trading on 1 March 2017 and prepared accounts for the period ended 31 December 2017. On 1 December 2017 she purchased a photocopier for £3,000 and a car with emissions of 125g/km for £3,000. The photocopier and the car are only used for business purposes.

The maximum capital allowances that Aasia will receive in respect of the purchase of the photocopier in the period ended 31 December 2017 are

A   £3,000
B   £2,500
C   £450

The maximum capital allowances that Aasia will receive in respect of the purchase of the car in the period ended 31 December 2017 are

D   £3,000
E   £540
F   £450

LO 3e

3   Leona began trading on 1 September 2017, preparing her first accounts to 31 December 2017. On 1 December 2017 she purchased a computer for £5,000 and a car with emissions of 125g/km for £13,200. Both assets are only used for business purposes.

The maximum capital allowances available on the computer in the period to 31 December 2017 are

A   £5,000
B   £1,667
C   £300

The maximum capital allowances available on the car in the period to 31 December 2017 are

D   £13,200
E   £2,376
F   £792

LO 3e

4   Barbara began trading on 1 January 2017. On 1 December 2017 Barbara purchased a van for £13,200. The van is used by her 80% of the time for business purposes and has CO_2 emissions of 120g/km.

What is the maximum capital allowance claim available to Barbara for the year ended 31 December 2017?

A   £1,901
B   £2,376
C   £10,560
D   £13,200   LO 3e

5   The following sentences have been included in a draft letter to a client who is about to start a new business.

Identify whether each statement is correct or incorrect.

Expenditure on new cars emitting CO_2 of not more than 75g/km qualifies for the annual investment allowance (AIA) of 100%.

A   Correct
B   Incorrect

Capital expenditure is not allowable in computing trading profits but will always result in capital allowances.

C   Correct
D   Incorrect   LO 3e

6   Murphy began trading on 1 January 2017 and drew up his first accounts to 31 December 2017.

He made the following purchases of assets.

		£
1 July 2017	Machinery	214,000
1 September 2017	Motor car (electric)	16,500

Murphy used the motor car only for business purposes.

What are Murphy's maximum capital allowances for the period ended 31 December 2017?

£ [   ]   LO 3e

7   Murray and Nuri have been trading in partnership for many years with a year end of 31 March.

The tax written down values of their assets at 1 April 2017 were:

		£
Murray's car – purchased 1 April 2011	Private use 40%, emissions 150g/km	17,000
Nuri's car – purchased 1 July 2011	Private use 30%, emissions 130g/km	8,000

Nuri's car was sold on 1 July 2017 for £6,000. Nuri intends to lease a car from this date.

What are the partnership's maximum capital allowances for the year ended 31 March '?

£ [   ]

LO 3e

8   Jack has been trading for many years making up accounts to 31 March.

The only asset in the business for the purpose of capital allowances is a car bought in 2012 with CO_2 emissions of 120g/km, which Jack uses 75% for business purposes. The tax written down value of the car at 1 April 2017 was £15,000.

On 1 September 2017 Jack sold the car for £10,200.

What are the maximum capital allowances available to Jack for the year ended 31 March '?

A   £2,025
B   £2,700
C   £3,600
D   £4,800   LO 3e

9   Mary, who runs a business, purchased the following assets in the year ended 31 December 2017.

		£
12 February 2017	Computer	10,000
20 March 2017	New car – emissions of 54g/km and used wholly for business purposes	8,000
1 May 2017	Office furniture	2,000

What are the maximum capital allowances available to Mary?

Capital allowances £ [   ]   LO 3e

10   Ming-Na began trading as a sole trader on 1 September 2017 preparing her first set of accounts for the nine months ended 31 May '.

On 1 November 2017 Ming-Na purchased a car with emissions of 130g/km for £18,000. She uses this 60% for business purposes.

What are the maximum capital allowances available for the car for the nine months ended 31 May '?

Capital allowances £ [   ]   LO 3e

11   Harry is a sole trader. In the year ended 31 March ' he sold a car for £14,500 which had a tax written down value brought forward at 1 April 2017 of £17,000. Harry used the car 70% for business purposes.

What is the balancing adjustment on disposal of the car in the year ended 31 March '?

A   Balancing allowance of £2,500
B   Balancing charge of £2,500
C   Balancing allowance of £1,750
D   Balancing charge of £1,750   LO 3e

12 Jack is a sole trader with accounts prepared to 31 May each year. In the year ended 31 May ' Jack purchased a car with emissions of 127g/km for £18,000. The car is driven by one of his employees who uses it 20% of the time for private purposes.

What is the maximum amount of capital allowances that can be claimed in the year ended 31 May ' relating to this car? £ [   ]   LO 3e

13 Pauline began trading as a sole trader on 1 October 2017, preparing her first set of accounts for the six months ended 31 March '. On the 1 January ' she purchased a new car with emissions of 125g/km for £16,000 (it is used only for business purposes).

What are the maximum amount of capital allowances Pauline may claim for the six months ended 31 March '?

A   £720
B   £1,440
C   £2,880
D   £16,000   LO 3e

14 Alex is a sole trader. He has plant and machinery with a tax written down value of £560 on 1 April 2017. During the nine-month accounting period to 31 December 2017, he purchased a computer for £8,000.

What are the maximum amount of capital allowances available to Alex for the nine months ended 31 December 2017?

A   £8,560
B   £8,076
C   £1,541
D   £1,156   LO 3e

15 Matthew is a sole trader and has prepared accounts for the year to 31 December 2017. At 1 January 2017 the business only owned one asset, a machine. The £12,000 cost of the machine had been put in the main pool when it was acquired several years ago. The balance on the main pool at 1 January 2017 was £2,300. The machine was sold on 30 June 2017 for £400. Matthew's business is continuing, but he now leases all machinery.

What are the maximum capital allowances that can be claimed by Matthew for the year ended 31 December 2017? £ [   ]   LO 3e

16 Max is a sole trader with a year ended 30 September 2017. The balance on the main pool at 1 October 2016 was £25,400. The only capital transaction was the disposal of a machine on 10 August 2017 for £4,300. The machine had cost £3,900 in April 2014.

What are the maximum capital allowances that can be claimed by Max for the year ended 30 September 2017? £ [   ]   LO 3e

17 Peter runs a business and prepared accounts for the six months to 31 March '. The tax written down value of the main pool at 1 October 2017 was £24,000. During the period of account, the following transaction took place.

	£
20 December 2017 Purchased new low emission car	9,000

What are the maximum capital allowances Peter may claim for the six months ended 31 March '?

A   £5,940
B   £9,000
C   £11,160
D   £13,320   LO 3e

18 Charlie, a sole trader, prepared accounts for the five months ended 31 December 2017. On 23 November 2017 he purchased a machine for £135,000.

What are the maximum capital allowances that can be claimed in respect of this machine for the period ended 31 December 2017?

A   £135,000
B   £87,208
C   £92,633
D   £83,333   LO 3e

19 Which of the following assets will **not** be in a single asset pool for capital allowance purposes?

A   Computer costing £10,000 with 30% private use by the owner of the business

B   Car with emissions of 125g/km costing £14,000 on 10 June 2017 with 20% private use by one of the employees

C   Car with emissions of 125g/km costing £13,000 on 1 January ' with 35% private use by the owner of the business

D   Delivery van costing £15,000 with 10% private use by the owner of the business   LO 3e

20 Jamie is a sole trader with a year ended 31 January '. The balance on the main pool at 1 February 2017 was £31,000. The only capital transaction was the disposal of a machine on 10 August 2017 for £5,300. The machine had originally cost £9,900.

What are the maximum capital allowances that can be claimed by Jamie for the year ended
31 January '? £ [   ]   LO 3e

21 Janice is a sole trader with a year ended 31 December 2017. On 1 May 2017 Janice bought a machine costing £220,000.

What are the maximum capital allowances that can be claimed by Janice on the machine for the year ended 31 December 2017? £ [   ]   LO 3e

Principles of Taxation: Question Bank

1   Rafael, Saeed and Tadeo have been in partnership for many years. The partnership agreement allocates a salary of £10,000 per annum to Saeed and all partners receive 5% per annum on their capital invested. The balance of any profits is shared equally.

During the year ended 30 June 2017 Rafael's capital account had a balance of £60,000, Saeed's balance was £24,000 and Tadeo's was £38,000. The partnership made trading profits of £125,000 in the year ended 30 June 2017.

What are the trading profits assessable on Rafael in 2017/18? £ [   ]   LO 3f

2   Townshend ceased trading on 30 November 2017. The recent tax-adjusted trading profits of his business are as follows.

	£
Year ended 30 April 2016	38,000
Year ended 30 April 2017	34,000
Period ended 30 November 2017	23,000

Townshend has unrelieved overlap profits of £7,000.

What is Townshend's trading profit assessment for 2016/17?

A   £38,000
B   £34,000
C   £34,334

What is Townshend's trading profit assessment for 2017/18?

D   £16,000
E   £50,000
F   £57,000   LO 3i

3   Jabir and Kadin began trading in partnership on 1 September 2017, sharing profits equally. The partnership agreement allocates an annual salary to Jabir of £8,000. For the year ended 31 August 2018 the partnership had a tax-adjusted trading profit of £105,000.

What are the partners' assessable trading profits for 2017/18?

A   Jabir £56,500   Kadin £48,500
B   Jabir £32,958   Kadin £28,292
C   Jabir £60,500   Kadin £52,500
D   Jabir £35,292   Kadin £30,625   LO 3f/3g

4   James started in business on 1 October 2017.

Which of the following will result in no overlap profits?

A   First accounts are year ended 30 September 2018 with future accounts to 30 September
B   First accounts are 6 months ended 5 April 2018 with future accounts to 5 April
C   First accounts are 3 months ended 31 December 2017 with future accounts to 31 December
D   First accounts are 4 months ended 31 January 2018 with future accounts to 31 January

LO 3g

5   Val, Cliff and Frank have been in partnership for many years preparing accounts to 30 September each year. The partnership agreement indicates that all partners receive 5% per annum on their capital invested. The balance of any remaining profits is shared equally.

During the year ended 30 September 2017 Val's capital account had a balance of £50,000, Cliff's balance was £30,000 and Frank's was £40,000. The partnership made trading profits of £150,000 in the year ended 30 September 2017.

What are the trading profits assessable on Cliff in 2017/18? £ [   ]   LO 3f

6   Tom and Dick have been trading in partnership for many years, sharing profits in the ratio 2:1. The partnership agreement allocates an annual salary to Tom of £10,000. The partnership had the following results.

Year ended 31 October 2017   £120,000
Year ended 31 October 2018   £150,000

What are the partners' assessable trading profits for 2017/18?

A   Tom £80,000   Dick £40,000
B   Tom £83,333   Dick £36,667
C   Tom £100,000   Dick £50,000
D   Tom £103,333   Dick £46,667   LO 3f

7   Raanan ceased trading on 31 December 2017. The recent tax-adjusted trading profits of his business are as follows.

	£
Year ended 31 January 2016	40,000
Year ended 31 January 2017	25,000
Period ended 31 December 2017	15,000

Raanan has unrelieved overlap profits of £8,000.

What is Raanan's trading profit assessment for 2017/18? £ [   ]   LO 3i

8   John started trading on 1 January 2016, but his business quickly ran into cash flow problems and he ceased to trade on 28 February 2018. The accounts for the year ended 31 December 2016 showed taxable trading profits of £6,000, and those for the period from 1 January 2017 to 28 February 2018 showed taxable trading profits of £2,800.

What is John's taxable trading profit for 2017/18?

A   £2,800
B   £2,400
C   £1,300
D   £900   LO 3g/3i

9   Trevor's business has unrelieved overlap profits brought forward of £4,000. He ceased trading on 30 April 2017. The recent tax-adjusted trading profits of his business are as follows.

	£
Year ended 30 September 2015	24,000
Year ended 30 September 2016	30,000
Period ended 30 April 2017	25,000

What are Trevor's taxable trading profits for 2017/18?

A   £55,000
B   £51,000
C   £25,000
D   £21,000   LO 3i

10 Obed began trading on 1 July 2017, preparing his first accounts to 30 June 2018. The adjusted trading profits for the year ended 30 June 2018 were £24,000.

What is Obed's assessable trading profit for 2017/18?

A   £6,000
B   £18,000
C   £20,000
D   £24,000   LO 3g

11 Nadeem began trading on 1 July 2017, preparing his first accounts to 30 June 2018. The adjusted trading profits for the year ended 30 June 2018 were £24,000.

What is Nadeem's overlap profit on commencement of trade?

A   £6,000
B   £18,000
C   £20,000
D   £24,000   LO 3g

12 Raeleen began trading on 1 January 2017, preparing her first accounts to 30 June 2017 and she will prepare them to every following June. The adjusted trading profits are as follows.

	£
6 months ended 30 June 2017	10,000
Year ended 30 June 2018 (estimated)	25,000

Which **two** of the following statements are correct?

A   Taxable trading profits for 2017/18 are £25,000.
B   Taxable trading profits for 2016/17 are £5,000.
C   Taxable trading profits for 2016/17 are £22,500.
D   Taxable trading profits for 2017/18 are £22,500.   LO 3g

13 Ben began trading on 1 January 2017, preparing his first accounts to 30 June 2018. The adjusted trading profits for the period ended 30 June 2018 were £42,000.

Which of the following statements is correct?

A   £28,000 is taxable in 2017/18, representing the period 6 April 2017 to 5 April 2018.
B   £28,000 is taxable in 2017/18, representing the year ended 30 June 2018.
C   £7,000 is taxable in 2017/18, representing the period 1 January 2017 to 5 April 2017.
D   £42,000 is taxable in 2017/18, representing the period to 30 June 2018.   LO 3g

14 Ray began trading on 1 July 2017, preparing his first accounts to 31 December 2017. The adjusted trading profits for the first two periods were

	£
6 m/e 31 December 2017	60,000
12 m/e 31 December 2018 (estimate)	100,000

What is the taxable trading income for 2017/18? £ [   ]   LO 3g

15 Ray began trading on 1 July 2017, preparing his first accounts to 31 December 2017. The adjusted trading profits for the first two periods were

	£
6 m/e 31 December 2017	60,000
12 m/e 31 December 2018 (estimate)	100,000

What are Ray's overlap profits? £ [   ]   LO 3g

16 Amber and Betty have been trading in partnership for many years, sharing profits in the ratio 2:1. On 1 July 2017 they changed the arrangement so that a salary of £20,000 pa is allocated to Amber and the remaining profits are shared equally. The partnership made adjusted trading profits of £240,000 in its year ended 31 December 2017.

What are the partners' assessable trading profits for 2017/18?

A   Amber £150,000   Betty £90,000
B   Amber £140,000   Betty £100,000
C   Amber £135,000   Betty £95,000
D   Amber £145,000   Betty £95,000   LO 3f

17 Aubrey and Elaine have been in partnership for many years. Both partners are allocated interest of 5% per annum on their capital invested. The balance of any profits is shared equally.

During the year ended 30 September 2017 Aubrey's capital account had a balance of £50,000, Elaine's was £20,000. The partnership made trading profits of £100,000 in the year ended 30 September 2017.

What are the trading profits assessable on Aubrey in 2017/18? £ [   ]   LO 3f

18 David and Doreen started in partnership together on 1 July 2017 sharing profits in the ratio 2:1. The partnership taxable trading profit for the year ended 30 June 2018 is £120,000.

What is the amount of trading profits taxable on Doreen in 2017/18?

A   £80,000
B   £60,000
C   £40,000
D   £30,000   LO 3f/3g

19 Florian ceased trading on 30 September 2017. The recent tax-adjusted trading profits of his business are as follows:

	£
Year ended 31 January 2016	28,500
Year ended 31 January 2017	21,200
Period ended 30 September 2017	17,430

Florian has unrelieved overlap profits of £2,610.

What is Florian's taxable trading income for 2017/18? £ [   ]

LO 3i

---

20 Leroy and Annabelle have been in partnership for many years. The partnership agreement allocates partners' interest at 5% pa on capital invested. The balance of any profit is shared in the ratio 2:3.

On 31 December 2016 Leroy's capital account had a balance of £35,000 and Annabelle's balance was £23,000. For the year ended 31 December 2017 the partnership had a tax-adjusted trading profit of £98,500.

What is Leroy's assessable trading profit for 2017/18?

A   £41,150
B   £39,990
C   £39,400
D   £38,240

LO 3f

---

21 Parminder began trading on 1 January 2017 making up her first set of accounts to 28 February 2018. Her tax-adjusted profits after capital allowances are as follows.

Period ended 28 February 2018   £53,208
Year ending 28 February 2019 £31,740 (estimate)

What is Parminder's taxable trading income for 2017/18?

A   £53,208
B   £45,607
C   £44,451
D   £31,740

LO 3g

---

22 Na is a sole trader and uses the cash basis. During the year to 30 April 2018 she had total receipts of £63,000. This included a receipt of £3,000 from the sale of a car.

Her payments for the year to 30 April 2018 totalled £27,000. This included interest paid of £600. At 30 April 2018 Na had prepaid rent on business premises of £1,000 relating to May and June 2018.

What is Na's taxable trading income for the year ended 30 April 2018? Ignore capital allowances.

A   £37,000
B   £33,000
C   £36,100
D   £33,100

LO 3e

23   Oscar started to trade as a sole trader on 1 July 2017 and has elected to use the cash basis for tax purposes. He has tax-adjusted total receipts for the 10 months ended 30 April 2018 of £58,000. He has tax-adjusted total payments for the period of £31,000.

What is Oscar's assessable trading profits for 2017/18?

A   £24,300
B   £27,000
C   £52,200
D   £58,000   LO 3e

Remember that when calculating NICs you should round mathematically at each step of the computation.

1   Sho has his own business and has tax-adjusted trading profits for the year of £6,100. He also has a part-time job earning £9,500 each year.

Which **two** of the following types of national insurance contributions must Sho pay for 2017/18?

A   Class 1 primary
B   Class 1 secondary
C   Class 2
D   Class 4   LO 1d

2   Robert, aged 59, is a director of Wagner Ltd, a company in which he owns 50% of the shares. He takes £50,000 a year out of the company, £20,000 as a salary and the balance as dividends.

The company employs George, aged 63, as Robert's personal assistant. His annual salary is £15,000.

The company makes a profit of £80,000 before tax and before accounting for the amounts paid to Robert.

Identify which of the following statements concerning NICs is/are correct.

Wagner Ltd will pay Class 4 NICs on the profits of £80,000.

A   Correct
B   Incorrect

George will pay Class 1 primary NICs on his earnings of £15,000.

C   Correct
D   Incorrect

Wagner Ltd will pay Class 1 secondary NICs on total employee remuneration of £65,000, before deducting the employment allowance.

E   Correct
F   Incorrect   LO 1d/3k

3   Steven has the following details for 2017/18.

	£
Salary from employment	15,000
Tax-adjusted trading profits after capital allowances	12,500

What are Steven's Class 4 national insurance contributions for 2017/18? £ [   ]   LO 3k

4   James has been trading for many years. His tax-adjusted trading profits for the last two years have been as follows.

	£
Year ended 5 April 2017	41,000
Year ended 5 April 2018	47,000

What are his Class 4 national insurance contributions for 2017/18?

A   £3,690
B   £3,355
C   £3,495
D   £2,955   LO 3k

5   Abe has been trading for many years. His adjusted trading profits for 2017/18 are £20,000.

What is Abe's total national insurance contributions liability for 2017/18?

A   £1,065
B   £1,213
C   £1,420
D   £1,568   LO 3k

6   During 2017/18 Ball Ltd pays Lena, one of its 25 employees, a salary of £38,862. The company provides her with a car that has a cash-equivalent benefit of £5,000 and supermarket vouchers which costs the company £500 pa.

What are the Class 1 secondary contributions payable by Ball Ltd in 2017/18 in respect of Lena?

£ [   ]

Ignore the employment allowance.   LO 3k

7   During 2017/18 Ball Ltd pays Lena, one of its 25 employees, a salary of £38,862. The company provides her with a car that has a cash-equivalent benefit of £5,000 and supermarket vouchers which cost the company £500 pa.

What are the Class 1A contributions payable by Ball Ltd in 2017/18 in respect of Lena?

£ [   ]

                                                                                                       LO 3k

8   Boris, aged 68, has a part-time job working for Jinx Ltd, earning £9,700 each year.

Identify whether the following statements are correct.

Boris will have Class 1 primary contributions deducted from his wages.

A   Correct
B   Incorrect

Jinx Ltd must pay Class 1 secondary contributions in relation to Boris's earnings.

C   Correct
D   Incorrect   LO 1d

9   Cobalt Ltd made a trading profit of £50,000 in its year ended 31 March 2018.

The company employs only a director, Bain, on an annual salary of £35,610.

What is the total national insurance liability of the company for 2017/18? £ [＿＿＿＿＿＿]   LO 3k

10 During 2017/18 Bat Ltd pays Larry a salary of £45,000 and provides him with benefits totalling £3,000.

What are the national insurance contributions payable by Bat Ltd in 2017/18 in respect of Larry?

A   £6,624
B   £4,834
C   £5,497
D   £5,083

Ignore the employment allowance.   LO 3k

11 During 2017/18 Trim Ltd pays Belinda a monthly salary of £3,300. In addition, Trim Ltd paid Belinda a bonus of £4,000 in December 2017.

What is Belinda's total national insurance contributions liability for 2017/18? £ [＿＿＿＿＿＿]

LO 3k

12 During 2017/18 Pirate Ltd pays Sue, aged 19, a salary of £47,000. The company provides her with a car that has a cash-equivalent benefit of £3,000.

What are the Class 1 secondary contributions payable by Pirate Ltd in 2017/18 in respect of Sue?
£ [＿＿＿＿＿＿]

Ignore the employment allowance.   LO 3k

13 During 2017/18 Pirate Ltd pays Sue, aged 19, a salary of £45,000. The company provides her with a car that has a cash-equivalent benefit of £3,000.

What are the Class 1A contributions payable by Pirate Ltd in 2017/18 in respect of Sue?
£ [＿＿＿＿＿＿]

LO 3k

14 Hans is a sole trader employing only one worker, Olga, on an annual salary of £36,000.

What are the Class 1 secondary contributions payable by Hans in 2017/18 in respect of Olga?
£ [＿＿＿＿＿＿]   LO 3k

15 During 2017/18 Rene Ltd pays Kamal, an apprentice aged 23, a salary of £20,000.

What are the Class 1 secondary contributions payable by Rene Ltd in 2017/18 in respect of Kamal?
£ [＿＿＿＿＿＿]

Ignore the employment allowance.   LO 3k

16 During 2017/18 Rene Ltd pays Kamal, an apprentice aged 23, a salary of £20,000.

What are the Class 1 primary contributions payable by Kamal in 2017/18? £ [   ] LO 3k

Chapter 9: Capital gains tax – individuals

1   The Quack partnership has recently disposed of an office building. The office building was owned jointly by all the partners. The office building was sold to a property developer.

   Who is liable to pay any capital gains tax due on the disposal of the office building?

   A   Partnership
   B   Partners jointly
   C   Property developer
   D   Partners individually   LO 1e/4a

---

2   Jamie entered into a contract with Annabelle to purchase a house. Contracts were exchanged on 15 March 2018. The contracts were completed and legal title therefore passed on 15 April 2018. Once contracts had been exchanged neither party could withdraw. Payment was not made until 17 April 2018 and Jamie did not physically move into the house until 18 April 2018.

   On what date will Annabelle be treated as having disposed of the house for capital gains tax purposes?

   A   15 March 2018
   B   15 April 2018
   C   17 April 2018
   D   18 April 2018   LO 1e

---

3   Which of the following statements about capital gains is true?

   A   Assets which are inherited are treated as being acquired by the donee at the price originally paid by the donor.

   B   Wasting chattels bought and sold for more than £6,000 are chargeable to CGT.

   C   Stamp duty land tax paid on the purchase of land may be deducted as part of cost on a subsequent disposal of the land.

   D   Where an asset is not sold at arm's length, the proceeds are deemed to equal cost so that no chargeable gain arises.   LO 4a/4b

---

4   Katie purchased an antique vase in January 1989 for £13,000. She sold it for £5,600 in March 2018 and paid auctioneer's fees of £800 for its sale.

   What is Katie's allowable loss on sale?

   A   £(7,800)
   B   £(8,200)
   C   £(7,400)
   D   £(7,000)   LO 4b

5   Freddy made two disposals during 2017/18.

For each of the two disposals select how the resulting gains should be treated to determine Freddy's total chargeable gains for 2017/18.

Gain of £4,500 on the disposal of a caravan.

A   Chargeable gain
B   Exempt

Gain of £1,000 on the sale of a sculpture. The sculpture originally cost £4,000.

C   Chargeable gain
D   Exempt

LO 4a

6   Thomas purchased an antique chair in February 2001 for £2,500. He sold it in May 2017 for £11,150. He paid £560 as commission to the agent who sold the chair for him.

What is the chargeable gain on the disposal of the chair?

A   £8,650
B   £8,583
C   £7,650
D   £8,090

LO 4b

7   David has net income for 2017/18 of £48,995. David has also made taxable gains of £33,422 for 2017/18.

Select how each of the following items will affect the calculation of David's capital gains tax liability for 2017/18, if at all.

His unused annual exempt amount from 2016/17

A   Reduces capital gains tax payable
B   Increases capital gains tax payable
C   No effect

Becoming a higher-rate taxpayer for the first time

D   Reduces capital gains tax payable
E   Increases capital gains tax payable
F   No effect

LO 4d

8   The Goose partnership has recently disposed of a chargeable asset. The chargeable asset was owned jointly by all the partners.

Who is liable to pay any capital gains tax due on the disposal of the chargeable asset?

A   Partners individually
B   No capital gains tax is due
C   Partnership
D   Partners jointly

LO 1e

9   In December 1997 Jasmine purchased a house for £176,000. Jasmine has always rented out the house to tenants. In December 2000 Jasmine installed a new bathroom at a cost of £6,400. In December 2017 Jasmine sold the house for £642,000. Jasmine also paid stamp duty land tax at 1% of the purchase price when she bought the house.

What is the chargeable gain on disposal of the house?

Chargeable gain £ _____   LO 4b

---

10 Jed purchased a rare painting in August 2004 for £3,200. He sold it in August 2017 for £14,150. He paid £142 as commission to the agent who sold the painting for him.

What is the chargeable gain on the disposal of the painting?

A   £10,808
B   £10,950
C   £13,583
D   £13,347   LO 4a/4b

---

11 Which **two** of the following items are exempt assets for capital gains tax purposes?

A   £15,000 of shares in an unquoted trading company
B   A diamond necklace purchased for £1,000 and now worth £17,000
C   A rare collection of snakes worth £320,000
D   £10,000 of National Savings Certificates   LO 4a

---

12 Which of the following disposals is a chargeable disposal for capital gains tax purposes?

A   Bequest of a house in the will of a mother to her daughter
B   Gift to a friend of £12,000 in National Savings Certificates
C   Gift to a friend of a painting worth £1,000,000
D   Gift of a painting to a charity when the painting was worth £300,000   LO 4a

---

13 Justin entered into a contract with Matthew to purchase a rare art collection. Contracts were exchanged on 1 August 2017 subject to an independent valuation being done. The valuation took place on 1 September 2017. Legal title finally passed on 5 September 2017. Payment was not made until 7 September 2017.

On what date will Matthew be treated as having disposed of the art collection for capital gains tax purposes?

A   1 August 2017
B   1 September 2017
C   5 September 2017
D   7 September 2017   LO 1e

14 Which of the following statements about capital gains is true?

    A   CGT is chargeable on individuals, partnerships and companies.

    B   Stamp duty land tax paid on the purchase of land may not be deducted as part of cost on a subsequent disposal of the land.

    C   Assets which are inherited are treated as being acquired by the donee at their value at the time of the donor's death.

    D   Where an asset is sold by an individual, indexation allowance will decrease the chargeable gain.

                                                                            LO 1e/4b

15 Harry made two disposals during 2017/18.

For each of the disposals, select how the resulting gains should be treated to determine Harry's total chargeable gains for 2017/18.

Gain of £2,500 on the disposal of a car.

    A   Chargeable gain
    B   Exempt

Gain of £3,000 on the sale of a greyhound, which originally cost £4,000.

    C   Chargeable gain
    D   Exempt   LO 4a

16 Which of the following does not pay tax on its chargeable gains?

    A   NSPCC, a registered charity
    B   WFT plc, a quoted company
    C   George and Bert, who are in partnership together
    D   Bert, in his own right as an individual   LO 4a

17 Which of the following is **not** a chargeable disposal made by Gordon?

    A   The sale of a building used by Gordon's business, to a third party
    B   The gift of shares to Gordon's son
    C   The loss of a painting valued at £50,000 during a fire at Gordon's house
    D   The gift of an antique table valued at £40,000 to Gordon's daughter on his death   LO 4a

18 Peter purchased a holiday home in July 2003. The holiday home cost £100,000 and he paid solicitor's fees of £2,500 relating to the purchase.

During 2004 he spent £2,800 on a garage for the holiday home and £580 on repairs to the plaster work when there was a flood. Peter anticipates selling the house within the next few months.

The total allowable expenditure on the disposal of the holiday home will be

    A   £100,000
    B   £102,500
    C   £105,300
    D   £105,880   LO 4b

19 Which **two** of the following are exempt wasting chattels for the purposes of capital gains tax.

    A   Office furniture, purchased for use only in Jack's business office on which he claims capital allowances

    B   A racehorse purchased as an investment by Max

    C   Goodwill of a computer manufacturing business with an expected life of 20 years

    D   A caravan, purchased by David for use on family holidays   LO 4a

20 Identify whether each of the following disposals will be chargeable or exempt.

Javier sold a painting at auction and received £5,900 after deducting auctioneers fees of £310. The painting had originally cost him £3,500.

    A   Chargeable
    B   Exempt

Savion received £2,600 for some shares that he sold after deducting £150 of fees. The shares originally cost him £800.

    C   Chargeable
    D   Exempt   LO 4a

21 Lourdes bought an antique brooch for £4,000 in October 2003. In January 2018, she sold it on the internet and received £6,200 after deduction of £100 fees.

What is Lourdes' chargeable gain?

    A   £333
    B   £500
    C   £2,200
    D   £2,300   LO 4b

22 In February 2004 Nuria purchased a painting for £6,700. She sold it at auction for £4,600 after deducting £200 of auctioneer's fees in October 2017.

What is the allowable loss on disposal?

    A   £(2,300)
    B   £(2,100)
    C   £(700)
    D   £(900)   LO 4b

23 Which of the following may result in a chargeable gain?

    A   A gift of a painting worth £250,000 to a local art gallery
    B   A sale of shares in Beagle plc by the RSPCA, a registered charity
    C   A gift of antique jewellery worth £25,000 by Robert, to his daughter as a wedding gift
    D   James sold gilt edged securities valued at £40,000 to his friend Arthur for £27,000   LO 4a

24 On which **two** of the following disposals must a chargeable gain/allowable loss be calculated?

    A   A sale of shares in Check plc by Cristiano. The shares were held in an ISA.

    B   Torey cashed in his National Savings Certificates in order to raise money for his wedding.

    C   Townsend lost an antique ring valued at £8,000 and received a cheque from the insurance company for that sum.

    D   Toshi sold a painting for £5,000. It was given to him several years ago when his grandfather died. At that time it was worth £6,400.

LO 4a

25 Fraser sold a diamond brooch at auction in June 2017, and received £7,900 after deduction of auctioneer's fees of £300. The brooch had cost him £6,100 in July 2000. Since then he had spent £250 in August 2001 having it cleaned and repaired. In September 2004 he paid £400 to have additional diamonds and rubies added to the brooch.

What is Fraser's chargeable gain on disposal of the brooch? £ _____

LO 4b

26 Identify whether each of the following disposals will be chargeable or exempt.

Erwin sold a painting at auction and received £6,100 after deducting auctioneer's fees of £200. The painting had originally cost him £3,500.

    A   Chargeable
    B   Exempt

Eryk received £5,900 for jewellery that he sold. The jewellery originally cost him £5,900 plus auctioneer's fees of £200.

    C   Chargeable
    D   Exempt

LO 4a

27 Ervin bought an antique vase for £4,000 in October 2005. In January 2018, he sold it for £6,300.

Assuming the annual exempt amount is used up by other disposals, Ervin's taxable gain on the vase is

    A   £0
    B   £500
    C   £2,000
    D   £2,300

LO 4b

28 In February 2004 Ebeneezer purchased a painting for £5,900. He sold it at auction for £5,600 after deducting £150 of auctioneer's fees in October 2017.

What is the allowable loss on disposal?

    A   £0
    B   £(300)
    C   £(50)
    D   £(150)

LO 4b

29 Which **two** of the following assets are exempt assets for capital gains tax purposes?

    A   An antique diamond necklace worth £3,000 (cost £2,500)
    B   A small hotel
    C   An oil painting worth £12,000 (cost £9,000)
    D   Fixed plant and machinery sold at a profit
    E   Shares held in an ISA   LO 4a

30 On 1 December 2017 David sold his holiday cottage for £200,000. He had bought the cottage in July 1999. The table below shows David's expenditure on the cottage prior to its sale.

Which **three** of these costs will be deducted in calculating David's chargeable gain?

A	Legal fees on purchase	£800
B	Purchase price	£110,000
C	Redecoration costs	£2,100
D	Cost of building a garage	£7,500
E	Replacement of a few roof tiles after a storm	£150

                                                                                        LO 4b

31 Martha has recently made two disposals. For each of the two disposals select how the resulting gains or losses should be treated in the computation of Martha's taxable gains.

Gain of £3,600 on the sale of goodwill in her ice cream van business.

    A   Chargeable gain
    B   Exempt

Loss of £2,000 on the sale of a diamond necklace which had cost £4,000.

    C   Allowable capital loss
    D   Exempt   LO 4a

32 Joshua has draft taxable gains of £30,500 for 2017/18 including the two items below. Select how Joshua's draft taxable gains will be affected by the correct treatment of each item.

A gain of £4,200 on the sale of his 10-year-old racehorse.

    A   No effect
    B   Increase
    C   Decrease

Auctioneer's fees of £500 have been deducted in arriving at the £13,400 gain on sale of an antique sculpture at an auction.

    D   No effect
    E   Increase
    F   Decrease   LO 4c

33 On 1 January 2018 Anna sold an office building for £500,000 before paying legal fees of £25,000. She had bought the building for £280,000 in July 2008.

Anna made no other disposals of chargeable assets during 2017/18. She had taxable income of £26,500 in 2017/18 after deduction of her personal allowance.

What is Anna's capital gains tax liability for 2017/18?

    A   £36,040
    B   £38,300
    C   £41,040
    D   £36,740   LO 4d

34   Becky sold a necklace for £56,000 in January 2018, incurring auctioneer's fees of £1,100. Becky had inherited the necklace from her mother on her mother's death in May 2005 when it was worth £20,000. Becky's mother had bought the necklace for £5,000 in January 1992.

Becky made no other disposals of chargeable assets during 2017/18. She had taxable income of £60,000 in 2017/18.

What is Becky's capital gains tax liability for 2017/18?

A   £4,720
B   £7,720
C   £4,940
D   £6,980

LO 4d

---

35   Jeremy has made two disposals. For each of the two disposals below, select how the gain or loss should be treated in the computation of Jeremy's taxable gains.

Gain of £13,000 on shares in an ISA.

A   Chargeable gain
B   Exempt

Loss of £3,000 on shares held directly by Jeremy which had cost £5,000.

C   Allowable capital loss
D   Exempt

LO 4a

---

36   Which of the following may result in a chargeable gain?

A   Sale of a vintage car for £20,000 which originally cost £12,000
B   Gift of cash of £50,000 from Jamil to his daughter to use as a house deposit
C   Sale for £5,000 of the goodwill of a trading business by Jack
D   Gift of premium bonds by Lisa to her daughter as a wedding gift

LO 4a

---

37   On 1 December 2017 Claire sold a painting for £50,200 which she had bought, unframed, from the artist for £8,000 in 2001. She had paid £2,000 to have the painting framed before sale.

Claire made no other disposals of chargeable assets during 2017/18. She had taxable income of £31,500 in 2017/18 after deduction of her personal allowance.

What is Claire's capital gains tax liability for 2017/18?

A   £5,980
B   £7,840
C   £5,780
D   £5,580

LO 4d

---

38   In March 1989, Matthew purchased an office for £642,000. Matthew sold the office in March 2018 for £1,250,400, incurring £120,000 estate agents' fees on the sale.

Matthew made no other disposals of chargeable assets during 2017/18. Matthew has taxable income of £29,130 in 2017/18 after deduction of his personal allowance.

What is Matthew's capital gains tax liability for 2017/18?

A   £97,243
B   £94,983
C   £95,420
D   £118,983

LO 4d

Chapter 10: Corporation tax

1   In January 1990, Sink Ltd purchased a property. In December 2001 Sink Ltd built an extension to the property. In September 2017 Sink Ltd sold the property.

What indexation factor should be used to calculate the indexation on the extension?

A   1.279
B   0.451
C   0.363
D   0.571

RPIs are as follows:

January 1990   119.5
December 2001   173.4
September 2017   272.4   LO 4b

2   Pineapple plc sold an antique writing desk which had been purchased in January 1996 for £18,000. It was sold for £3,200 in January 2018. The proceeds were received net of selling fees of £400.

What is Pineapple plc's allowable loss?

A   £(12,000)
B   £(12,400)
C   £(15,200)
D   £(26.224)

RPIs are as follows:

January 1996   150.2
January 2017   265.5   LO 4b

3   Shower plc has made two disposals in its year ended 31 August 2018.

For each of the two disposals select how the resulting gains should be treated in the calculation of Shower plc's chargeable gains.

Gain of £24,000 on the disposal of a rare African snake which had not been used in the business.

A   Chargeable gain
B   Exempt

Gain of £1,100 on the sale of an antique chair. The chair originally cost £5,000.

C   Chargeable gain
D   Exempt   LO 4a

4   Pasta plc sold one of its warehouses on 1 July 2017 for £2,125,000. The warehouse originally cost £432,000 in February 1986. On disposal Pasta plc paid estate agents fees of £24,969. At acquisition legal fees were £3,000 and stamp duty land tax was £12,960. During its ownership Pasta plc added a canteen to the building at a cost of £48,000.

What is Pasta plc's unindexed gain on this disposal?

Unindexed gain £ [   ]

LO 4b

5   Pumpkin Ltd purchased a plot of land in August 1991 for £60,000. The company sold it in November 2017, incurring £750 for advertising.

What is the indexation allowance relating to the disposal?

A   £62,520
B   £62,506
C   £61,738
D   £63,302

RPIs are as follows:

August 1991   134.1
November 2017   273.8

LO 4b

6   Party Ltd purchased a building for investment purposes in March 1996 for £150,000. The company sold it in September 2017 for £425,000. The indexation factor to apply to the disposal is 0.814.

What is the gain in Party Ltd's corporation tax computation for the year ended 31 December 2017?

A   £0
B   £275,000
C   £51,150
D   £152,900

LO 4b

7   Which of the following statements is correct?

A   For individuals and companies there is an annual exempt amount available to reduce the amount of gains taxable each year.

B   Individuals and partnerships will be able to reduce their gains by indexation allowance.

C   Capital gains tax is payable by individuals and companies on their taxable gains.

D   Individuals will have a chargeable gain on disposal of goodwill from their business.   LO 1d/4b

8   Tractor Ltd realised a chargeable gain of £16,000 on disposal of a building in January 2018.

What is the tax suffered by Tractor Ltd on its chargeable gain?

A   £470
B   £893
C   £3,040
D   £1,600

LO 4c

9   Lettuce Ltd was incorporated on 11 May 2017. It opened an interest bearing building society account on 1 July 2017 and began trading on 1 January 2018. It will make up its first set of accounts to 30 September 2018 and annually thereafter.

What are the dates of Lettuce Ltd's first accounting period for corporation tax purposes?

A   11 May 2017 – 31 December 2017
B   1 July 2017 – 31 December 2017
C   1 January 2018 – 30 September 2018
D   1 January 2018 – 31 December 2018   LO 5a

10   Which of the following statements about corporation tax is true?

A   A company which is centrally managed and controlled in the UK will always be liable to UK corporation tax on its worldwide profits.

B   A company which is incorporated in the UK will only be liable to UK corporation tax on its worldwide profits if it is also centrally managed and controlled in the UK.

C   A company which is incorporated abroad and centrally managed and controlled abroad, will still be liable to UK corporation tax on its worldwide profits.

D   A company which is incorporated abroad will never be liable to UK corporation tax on its worldwide profits.   LO 5d

11   Airedale Ltd was incorporated on 11 June 2017. It opened an interest bearing building society account on 1 August 2017 and began trading on 1 February 2018. It makes up its first set of accounts to 30 September 2018 and annually thereafter.

What are the dates of Airedale Ltd's first accounting period for corporation tax purposes?

A   1 August 2017 – 31 July 2018
B   11 June 2017 – 31 January 2018
C   1 February 2018 – 30 September 2018
D   1 August 2017 – 31 January 2018   LO 5a

12   Papillon Ltd has taxable total profits of £350,000 for its three-month accounting period to 31 December 2017.

What is Papillon Ltd's corporation tax liability for the three months ended 31 December 2017?

Papillon Ltd's corporation tax liability £ [   ]   LO 5d

13   Jaffrey Ltd is a UK-resident trading company that made various disposals during the year ended
     31 March 2018.

     Select how the resulting gains or losses should be treated in the corporation tax computation of
     Jaffrey Ltd for the year ended 31 March 2018.

     Loss of £5,900 on the sale of two cars used in the business. Each car cost and was sold for more
     than £6,000.

     A   Chargeable gain
     B   Exempt
     C   Allowable capital loss

     Gain of £86,000 on the sale of an investment property.

     D   Chargeable gain
     E   Exempt
     F   Allowable capital loss   LO 4a

14   Ardent Ltd bought a factory on 12 February 1996 for £165,000. At acquisition, professional fees
     were £2,450 and stamp duty land tax was £1,650. In May 2001 an extension was added to the
     factory at a cost of £23,000.

     In October 2017 Ardent Ltd sold the factory, which had always been used in its trade, for
     £312,000. Prior to the sale, Ardent Ltd repaired water damage on one wall at a total cost of
     £3,000.

     What is the unindexed gain on the sale of the factory?

     Unindexed gain £ [   ]   LO 4b

15   Rhodes Ltd has taxable total profits for the nine-month period ended 31 March 2018 of
     £1,088,600.

     What is the corporation tax payable by Rhodes Ltd for the period ended 31 March 2018?

     Corporation tax payable £ [   ]   LO 5d

16   Lam Ltd began trading on 1 February 2016 and had the following periods of account:

     1 February 2016 to 31 July 2017

     1 August 2017 to 30 April 2018 (when the trade ceased)

     Its first corporation tax accounting period was

     A   1 February 2016 to 31 July 2016
     B   1 February 2016 to 31 January 2017
     C   1 February 2016 to 30 April 2017
     D   1 February 2016 to 31 July 2017   LO 5a

17   Jam Ltd has taxable total profits of £260,000 for the year ended 31 December 2017.

     What is the corporation tax payable by Jam Ltd for the year ended 31 December 2017?

     Corporation tax payable £ [   ]   LO 5d

1   Clementine orders some goods from Forty-Niner plc on 1 May. They are dispatched on 8 May. On 4 June Clementine receives the respective invoice dated 2 June. Her payment arrives at the company on 7 June. Forty-Niner plc does not operate the cash accounting scheme.

Which of the following options is the tax point for the transaction?

A   1 May
B   8 May
C   2 June
D   7 June   LO 6d

2   Matilda has been a VAT-registered trader for a number of years and has recently purchased various items for use in her trade.

Select the item on which Matilda **cannot** recover the input tax.

A   Van accessories purchased a year ago
B   Fixed partitions for use in the office
C   A motorcycle for business deliveries
D   Entertaining costs of UK business customers   LO 6e

3   James, a trader, wishes to register voluntarily for VAT.

What must James do, in addition to notifying HMRC, in order to be VAT-registered?

A   Demonstrate to HMRC that he intends to make either zero or standard-rated supplies or both
B   Demonstrate to HMRC that he will make only zero-rated supplies
C   Demonstrate to HMRC that he will make only exempt supplies
D   Demonstrate to HMRC that his sole intention for registering is to recover input tax   LO 6c

4   Bob, who is not registered for VAT, has just completed 12 months' trading, the turnover details for the past year being as follows.

	£
Exempt supplies	28,000
Standard-rated supplies	58,000
Zero-rated supplies	29,000

Which of the following options correctly identifies Bob's liability to register for VAT?

A   He is not required to register
B   He must register, based on turnover of exempt and standard-rated supplies
C   He must register, based on turnover of standard and zero-rated supplies
D   He must register, based on turnover of exempt, standard and zero-rated supplies   LO 6c

5 Charles, a VAT-registered trader, invoices Bronco Ltd in November 2017 for standard-rated supplies of £1,000, excluding VAT.

The following settlement discounts are offered.

Payment within	Discount
7 days	10%
14 days	5%
21 days	2.5%

Bronco Ltd, whose normal credit term is 21 days, agrees beforehand to settle the invoice within 14 days, but actually takes 28 days.

How much VAT is Bronco Ltd required to pay?

A £180
B £195
C £190
D £200

LO 6e

---

6 Viking Raiders Ltd began trading on 1 January 2017. Details of the company's recent taxable turnover are as follows.

2017	£	2018 (forecast figures)	£
January	720	January	12,970
February	1,220	February	13,960
March	2,250	March	10,770
April	2,490	April	11,860
May	3,890		
June	4,620		
July	5,870		
August	5,890		
September	5,920		
October	7,170		
November	9,800		
December	10,270		

By what date must Viking Raiders Ltd notify HMRC of its liability to register?

A 28 February 2018
B 30 March 2018
C 31 March 2018
D 1 April 2018

LO 6c

---

7 Paint Ltd incurred the following capital expenditure (including VAT).

	£	
New car for salesman	12,810	(80% business use)
New motor van	9,450	
Second-hand container lorry	23,100	

How much VAT can be reclaimed in respect of the above?

A £3,850
B £5,425
C £7,133
D £7,560

LO 6e

8   Where a supply is made, a taxable person can, in respect of a default by a debtor, claim a refund of the relevant VAT if certain conditions are fulfilled.

Which of the following options is **not** one of the conditions required?

A   The debtor must be formally insolvent.
B   A period of six months must have elapsed since the time of the supply and due date of payment.
C   Output tax on the supply has been accounted for and paid.
D   The debt has been written off as a bad debt in the accounts.   LO 6e

9   Tariq ordered some goods from Rumpole Ltd, which issued a VAT invoice on 1 February. As payment for the goods, Tariq sent a cheque which Rumpole Ltd received on 3 February. The goods were dispatched on 8 February and received by Tariq on 10 February. Rumpole Ltd is not a member of the cash accounting scheme.

Which of the following options is the tax point for the supply?

A   1 February
B   3 February
C   8 February
D   10 February   LO 6d

10   Quentin, who is registered for VAT, supplies computer hardware and related support services.

On 28 March 2018 he gave a new laptop to his sister. The laptop cost the business £2,500 (excluding VAT) in January 2018 but the same model could have been purchased for £2,000 on 28 March 2018 (excluding VAT).

How much output VAT should Quentin include in his VAT return in respect of the above transaction?

A   £333.33
B   £400.00
C   £416.67
D   £500.00   LO 6e

11   Valerie is a sole trader running two separate businesses – a wholesale fabric business and a clothes retail business. She is also senior partner in a firm of interior designers. All three businesses have a taxable turnover in excess of £100,000.

What is the maximum number of VAT registrations to which Valerie will be a party?

A   One
B   Two
C   Three
D   She may elect for two or three   LO 6c

12 Cross plc issues an invoice for standard-rated goods in February 2018 as follows.

	£
Goods excluding VAT	1,800
Less trade discount	(180)
Cash discount (only available if the invoice is settled within 30 days)	(108)
Cash to pay within 30 days	1,512

How much VAT will be paid overall if the customer pays within 30 days?

A   £360.00
B   £338.40
C   £302.40
D   £324.00

LO 6e

13 Priti purchases goods from Kuldip as follows.

1   Kuldip receives payment for goods on 4 May
2   Kuldip dispatches the goods on 8 May
3   Priti receives the goods on 12 May
4   Kuldip issues an invoice on 17 May

Kuldip does not operate the cash accounting scheme.

What is the tax point for this supply?

A   4 May
B   8 May
C   12 May
D   17 May

LO 6d

14 Priscilla started trading in the winter of 2016 but did not register for VAT because she expected that her turnover would be below the registration limits. On 31 May 2017 she realised that her future taxable turnover would exceed £85,000 in the next 30 days alone.

By what date must Priscilla notify HMRC that she is liable to be registered for VAT?

A   31 May 2017
B   29 June 2017
C   1 July 2017

From what date must Priscilla charge VAT on her taxable supplies?

D   31 May 2017
E   30 June 2017
F   1 July 2017

LO 6c

15 Paola, who is registered for VAT, runs a chauffeur-driven car hire service. In the quarter ended 31 March 2018 she lent a car and chauffeur to her cousin, to drive him to the airport. In the same quarter Paola arranged for a car and chauffeur to drive her to the church for her wedding.

Which of these, if any, will be treated as a supply of services for VAT purposes?

A   Neither
B   Loan of car to her cousin only
C   Use of car for her wedding only
D   Both

LO 6a

16 Diane, a VAT-registered trader who is not a member of the cash accounting scheme, supplies some goods to a customer. The goods are dispatched on 27 March. Diane's VAT accounting period ends on 31 March. An invoice is issued on 2 April and payment is received on 4 April.

What is the tax point?

A   27 March
B   31 March
C   2 April
D   4 April   LO 6d

17 Walton Ltd, a manufacturing company which is registered for VAT, purchased a motor car for £10,470 (which included £160 for vehicle excise duty) inclusive of VAT. The car is used by one of the employees for business and private use.

What amount should be included in the capital allowance computation as the acquisition cost of this vehicle?

A   £8,592
B   £8,725
C   £10,310
D   £10,470   LO 6b

18 Which of the following is always a condition which must be fulfilled if input tax on the purchase of goods from a VAT-registered person is to be recovered?

A   Payment has been made for the goods
B   A tax invoice is held
C   The supplier has been paid
D   The goods have been resold to a customer   LO 6e

19 Chris, who is registered for VAT, runs a large computer programming business in Stafford. During the quarter ended 30 June 2017 he spent £240 on his lunches taken locally and £480 on his lunches taken in Cornwall while staying away from home on business trips there. Both figures include VAT.

How much VAT may Chris claim as input tax?

A   £0
B   £40
C   £80
D   £120   LO 6e

20 Parminder runs two separate businesses. The first business is a clothes repair service which has taxable supplies of £35,000 per annum. The second business is a carwash service which has taxable supplies of £245,000 per annum. Both businesses are run by Parminder as a sole trader.

Which of the businesses is relevant in determining whether Parminder should register for VAT?

A   Both businesses
B   The clothes repair service
C   The car-wash service
D   Neither business   LO 6c

21 Sheep plc began trading on 1 December 2017. On 1 February 2018 it won a contract to supply goods on 15 February 2018 worth £350,000.

By what date must Sheep plc notify HMRC that it is liable to be registered for VAT?

A   28 February
B   2 March
C   17 March

From what date must Sheep plc charge VAT on its taxable supplies?

D   1 February
E   28 February
F   1 March   LO 6c

22 Cow plc has been trading for many years and has always been VAT registered. On 1 March 2018 it ceased to make zero-rated supplies. Cow plc is now a wholly exempt trader with annual supplies of £86,000 on average.

What action must Cow plc now take in relation to its VAT registration?

A   No action need be taken as the company is still making supplies in excess of £83,000
B   Deregistration will be effective immediately and must be notified by 2 March 2018
C   Deregistration will be effective immediately and must be notified by 30 March 2018
D   No action need be taken as the company is still making supplies in excess of £81,000   LO 6c

23 Gobble plc made the following two standard-rated supplies during July 2017:

Clothes (exclusive of VAT)	£400
Material (inclusive of VAT)	£514

What is the total amount of output VAT collected?

A   £169.47
B   £165.67
C   £182.80
D   £152.33   LO 6e

24 In December 2017, Moo plc makes a standard-rated supply of goods and issues an invoice for £1,000 plus VAT to Ferdinand. A 4% discount is offered if payment is received within 17 days of the invoice date. Ferdinand took 16 days to pay.

What is the correct amount of output VAT paid by Ferdinand overall? £ [   ]   LO 6e

25 From the following list of purchases, select **two** items for which the input VAT is **always** wholly irrecoverable.

A   UK client entertaining
B   Fuel in company pool cars
C   Capital item still used exclusively for business use but purchased two months pre-registration
D   Gifts of goods to customers
E   Company car for employee use which is a taxable benefit for income tax purposes   LO 6e

26 In his first year of trading to 31 December 2016 Wayne's taxable turnover from his business was £3,700 each month.

For the first seven months of 2017 his taxable turnover was as follows:

	£
January 2017	6,100
February 2017	7,800
March 2017	8,500
April 2017	12,400
May 2017	13,700
June 2017	14,900
July 2017	13,000

By what date must Wayne notify HMRC of his liability to register for VAT?

A   30 May 2017
B   30 June 2017
C   30 July 2017
D   30 August 2017   LO 6c

27 Benedict began trading on 1 August 2017 repairing electrical equipment and applied to register for VAT with effect from 1 December 2017. Prior to registration he had incurred VAT as follows.

	£
Van purchased on 3 May 2017 still in use at 30 November 2017	500
Accountancy fees on invoice dated 5 September 2017	30
Stock of spare parts as at 30 November 2017	240

How much VAT can Benedict reclaim in respect of these items?

A   £770
B   £740
C   £270
D   £240   LO 6e

28 Which of the following statements about VAT is true?

A   A trader who makes only exempt supplies may register for VAT.

B   VAT is charged on zero-rated supplies.

C   VAT on standard-rated supplies is always charged at 5%.

D   A trader making taxable supplies may only register for VAT once supplies exceed the VAT registration threshold.   LO 6b/6c

29 Michael began trading as a cabinet maker on 1 October 2016. His quarterly turnover (spread evenly over the quarter) is as follows.

Quarter ended	£
31 December 2016	12,000
31 March 2017	13,200
30 June 2017	19,500
30 September 2017	26,700
31 December 2017	32,700
31 March 2018	35,000

By what date must Michael notify HMRC of his liability to register for VAT?

A 30 December 2017
B 31 December 2017
C 30 January 2018
D 31 January 2018

LO 6c

30 Miranda's taxable sales have dropped to £30,000 pa and forecast annual sales are expected to be between £30,000 and £40,000.

Which of the following options correctly identifies the VAT implications for Miranda?

A Miranda must deregister and will need to pay output VAT on the deemed supply of stock and capital items still held at deregistration.

B Miranda must deregister and will need to pay output VAT on the deemed supply of stock and capital items still held at deregistration where the output VAT exceeds £1,000.

C Miranda may choose to deregister but would then need to pay output VAT on the deemed supply of stock and capital items still held at deregistration if the output VAT exceeds £1,000.

D Miranda may choose to deregister but would then need to pay output VAT on the deemed supply of stock and capital items still held at deregistration.

LO 6c

31 Which of the following is **not** a deemed supply for VAT purposes?

A Sale of goods on hire purchase
B Gifts of business assets worth £100 each to a customer
C Gifts of services worth £100 to a customer
D Drawings of stock by the proprietor of a business

LO 6a

32 Kevin is a VAT-registered trader who has suffered input tax as follows on purchases in the past month.

	£
Television for Kevin's wife	350
Machine for business use (Kevin has lost the VAT receipt)	989
Office stationery	256

How much input tax may Kevin recover on these items?

A £256
B £989
C £1,245
D £1,595

LO 6e

33 Which of the following statements about VAT is true?

    A   Where discounts are offered VAT should be calculated based on those discounts offered, rather than actually obtained.

    B   A gift of business services is not a taxable supply.

    C   A supply of a business asset used for private purposes is not a taxable supply.

    D   Input VAT is recoverable on company cars to the extent they are used for business purposes.

LO 6b/6e

34 Flight plc is VAT-registered but is not a member of the cash accounting scheme. A major customer of Flight plc went into liquidation today and there is little hope of its debt being recovered. The invoice was issued on 1 August 2017 with a credit agreement of payment by the end of the month. The associated output VAT was paid to HMRC in the quarter ended 31 October 2017 return. The debt will be written off in Flight plc's accounts on 31 March 2018.

Assuming it is now 1 January 2018, what is the earliest date the output VAT could be reclaimed from HMRC?

    A   1 January 2018
    B   1 February 2018
    C   28 February 2018
    D   31 March 2018

LO 6e

35 Sunil ordered some goods from Grumpy Ltd, which issued a VAT invoice on 1 September. Sunil sent a cheque for the goods which Grumpy Ltd received on 3 September. The goods were dispatched on 8 September and received by Sunil on 10 September. Grumpy Ltd is not a member of the cash accounting scheme.

What is the tax point for the supply?

    A   1 September
    B   3 September
    C   8 September
    D   10 September

LO 6d

36 Tien orders some goods on sale or return from Spice Ltd on 1 October. They are dispatched on 9 October. Tien adopts the goods on 1 November. Tien then receives the invoice for the goods dated 20 November. Spice Ltd receives payment for the goods on 29 December. Tien and Spice Ltd are not members of the cash accounting scheme.

What is the actual tax point of the transaction?

    A   1 October
    B   9 October
    C   1 November
    D   20 November

LO 6d

37 Ahsan orders some goods from Land Ltd on 1 October. They are dispatched on 18 October. Ahsan then receives the invoice for the goods dated 29 October. Land Ltd receives payment for the goods on 7 December. Ahsan is not a member of the cash accounting scheme.

What is the actual tax point of the transaction?

A   1 October
B   18 October
C   29 October
D   7 December   LO 6d

38 Disco Ltd intends to register voluntarily for VAT.

Which of the following statements is correct?

A   Disco Ltd must be expecting to be in a repayment position.
B   Disco Ltd must not be making any exempt supplies.
C   Disco Ltd must be making or intending to make some taxable supplies.
D   Disco Ltd must be expecting to exceed the VAT threshold within the next 12 months.   LO 6c

39 Tambourine Ltd makes standard-rated supplies. At the end of October 2017 its taxable turnover in the previous 12 months exceeds £85,000 for the first time. Its turnover is expected to rise gradually.

The company is required to notify HMRC of its liability to register by

A   1 November 2017
B   30 November 2017
C   1 December 2017

Registration takes effect from

D   1 November 2017
E   30 November 2017
F   1 December 2017   LO 6c

40 Arthur, who is not registered for VAT, has just completed 12 months' trading. The turnover for the trading year is as follows.

	£
Exempt supplies	14,300
Taxable supplies	69,250

Additionally Arthur sold an item of machinery (standard rated) for £14,000.

Based on the above information, does Arthur have any liability to register for VAT?

A   Yes, based on exempt and taxable supplies of normal trading
B   Yes, based on taxable supplies of normal trading, plus the sale of machinery
C   No, based on taxable supplies of normal trading
D   Yes, based on exempt and taxable supplies of normal trading, plus the sale of machinery

LO 6c

41 Abida is a salesman who incurred the following expenditure during his work.

	Net £	VAT £	Gross £
Hotel accommodation reimbursed to him by his employers	320	64	384
Meals paid out of his salary	200	40	240

In addition his employer purchased a laptop computer for Abida to use as an essential part of his job. The employer agreed 10% personal use for this equipment which had cost £1,080 (including VAT of £180).

How much may be shown as net deductible input tax on the employer's VAT return?

A   £226
B   £244
C   £266
D   £284

LO 6e

42 Books Ltd incurred the following capital expenditure (including VAT).

	£
Car for salesman used for business and private purposes	15,750
Delivery van	10,080

How much VAT can be reclaimed in respect of the above?

A   £2,016
B   £1,680
C   £2,625
D   £4,305

LO 6e

43 Identify whether the following are correct conditions for the reclaim of output tax as bad debt relief.

A period of six months has elapsed since the goods were supplied.

A   Correct
B   Incorrect

Tax on the supply has been accounted for and paid.

C   Correct
D   Incorrect

The bad debt claim must be made within six years of becoming eligible for relief.

E   Correct
F   Incorrect

LO 6e

44   Music Ltd has just received the following invoice from a supplier with a delivery of equipment (all figures exclude VAT).

	£
Musical equipment	6,400
Less 10% discount for settlement within 14 days	(640)
Cash to pay if settled within 14 days	5,760

If payment is made within 21 days the discount is reduced to 5%.

Music Ltd has a policy of paying one week after being invoiced.

What is the correct amount of VAT that Music Ltd will pay?

   A   £960
   B   £1,152
   C   £1,216
   D   £1,280

LO 6e

45   Peter purchases goods from John. Peter paid for the goods when he ordered them on 3 April. John made the goods available to Peter on 7 April, but Peter did not collect them until 11 April. John issued the invoice on 16 April.

What is the actual tax point for this supply?

   A   3 April
   B   7 April
   C   11 April
   D   16 April

LO 6d

46   Identify whether each of the following is a taxable supply for VAT purposes.

Steve, who is registered for VAT, runs a plant hire company. In the quarter ended 31 March 2018 he let his brother use a digger at no charge.

   A   Taxable
   B   Not taxable

In the quarter to 30 June 2018 he used the same digger to help dig the foundations for the extension being built onto his house.

   C   Taxable
   D   Not taxable

LO 6a

47   Block Ltd, a building company which is registered for VAT, purchased a motor car for use by the sales director for £25,380 (including £705 for the factory fitted satellite navigation), inclusive of VAT. The car is used 20% privately by the sales director.

What is the cost to the company of the vehicle for capital allowance purposes?

   A   £25,380
   B   £24,675
   C   £21,150
   D   £20,563

LO 6b

48 Charlie has a shop selling women's clothing. She gave a coat that she had bought for £120 to her sister. She would have sold the coat in the shop for £200. All figures are VAT-inclusive.

What is the value of the coat for VAT purposes?

A   £200.00
B   £166.67
C   £120.00
D   £100.00

LO 6b

49 Gertrude has a quarter ended 31 March 2018. Her normal payment terms are one calendar month after invoice date. Identify whether bad debt relief can be claimed in respect of the following amounts owed to Gertrude as at 31 March 2018.

Wood Ltd still owes £5,000 from an invoice issued on 30 June 2017. Gertrude still believes that the amount will be paid in full and so it has not been written off in the accounts.

A   Bad debt relief can be claimed
B   Bad debt relief cannot be claimed

Trees Ltd owes £2,000 from an invoice issued on 15 September 2017. Gertrude does not expect payment of this debt and has written it off in the accounts.

C   Bad debt relief can be claimed
D   Bad debt relief cannot be claimed

LO 6e

50 Jacob, who is VAT-registered, opened a new shop selling electrical supplies. He took goods valued at £230 for use in his own house and sent out a sample worth £12 to each of 200 potential new customers.

Which of the following statements is correct?

A   Only the goods used in Jacob's house are a taxable supply.
B   Only the samples sent to potential customers are a taxable supply.
C   Both are taxable supplies.
D   Neither are taxable supplies.

LO 6a

51 Identify whether each of the following statements is correct.

A business making £48,000 of standard-rated supplies and £38,000 of exempt supplies is required to register for VAT.

A   Correct
B   Incorrect

A business making £86,000 of zero-rated supplies only does not have to become VAT registered.

C   Correct
D   Incorrect

LO 6c

52   Lancashire Ltd began trading on 1 January 2017. The company's taxable turnover was £4,900 per month for the first six months, rising to £7,700 per month for the next six months. In January 2018 the turnover increased to £14,400 per month.

Lancashire Ltd must start to charge VAT on its supplies from

A   31 January 2018
B   28 February 2018
C   1 March 2018
D   2 March 2018   LO 6c

53   Yorks Ltd began trading on 1 January 2018, anticipating taxable turnover of £86,000 per month.

It must notify HMRC of its liability to register for VAT by

A   1 January 2018
B   30 January 2018
C   31 January 2018

The company's VAT registration is effective from

D   1 January 2018
E   30 January 2018
F   31 January 2018   LO 6c

54   Maddie is registered for VAT and makes standard-rated supplies only. Maddie sold some goods to Julie for £76 without charging any VAT because Maddie believed that the goods were exempt from VAT.

Maddie has now discovered that VAT should have been charged on this sale.

How much VAT is payable on this sale and by whom?

The amount of VAT payable is

A   £12.67
B   £15.20

The VAT is payable by

C   Maddie
D   Julie   LO 1d/6e

55 Harry began trading on 1 September 2017. His monthly turnover for the first 18 months of trade is as follows.

Turnover	Per month (excluding VAT) £
Standard-rated supplies	4,600
Zero-rated supplies	1,900
Exempt supplies	500
	6,000

On 1 May 2017, Harry sold surplus office machinery for £3,500 (excluding VAT).

Select whether the following supplies should be included in order to determine when the VAT registration limit of £85,000 is first exceeded by Harry's business.

Exempt supplies

A Include
B Do not include

Supply of surplus office machinery

C Include
D Do not include   LO 6c

---

56 Skating Ltd is a VAT-registered company that only makes standard-rated supplies.

Select the extent to which the input tax is recoverable on the following VAT-inclusive costs incurred by Skating Ltd.

£15,000 for the purchase of a new machine. The VAT invoice has been lost and cannot be replaced.

A Fully recoverable
B Partially recoverable
C Not recoverable

Purchase of a car for a salesman for £20,000. The car is used 60% for business purposes.

D Fully recoverable
E Partially recoverable
F Not recoverable   LO 6e

---

57 Jack is a VAT-registered trader making only standard-rated supplies. Jack received an order from a customer on 20 February 2018 and dispatched the goods on the same day. Included with the order was payment of a 10% deposit of £1,150 including VAT.

An invoice for the full amount of £11,500 including VAT was issued on 1 March 2018. The balancing payment of £10,350 was received on 10 April 2018.

Assuming that Jack does not operate the cash accounting scheme, calculate how much output tax (to the nearest £1) must be accounted for on the following VAT returns:

Quarter to 28 February 2018

A £0
B £192
C £1,150

Quarter to 31 May 2018

D £0
E £1,725
F £1,917   LO 6e

58 David is registered for VAT. David sold goods to George for £100 without charging any VAT. George had assured him that the goods were exempt from VAT. David later discovered that the standard rate of VAT should have been charged on this sale.

The amount of VAT payable is

A   £16.67
B   £20.00

The VAT is payable by

C   David
D   George

LO 1d/6e

59 Which **two** of the following statements are correct in relation to registering for VAT?

A   A trader can voluntarily register for VAT if he makes only exempt supplies.

B   A trader can voluntarily register for VAT if he makes only zero-rated supplies.

C   A trader making both zero-rated and standard-rated supplies is required to register only if the level of taxable supplies exceeds the VAT registration limit.

D   A trader making exempt supplies must register for VAT if his supplies exceed the VAT registration limit.

LO 6c

60 Branimir is registered for VAT and is preparing his VAT return for the three-month period ended 31 March 2018. During this period he made zero-rated supplies of £23,000 and standard-rated supplies of £29,560. These figures are VAT exclusive.

Branimir incurred input tax related to the zero-rated supplies of £2,130 and input tax related to the standard-rated supplies of £900. Branimir also paid salaries of £5,800 for the three-month period which relate to the business as a whole.

How much output VAT should Branimir account for on his VAT return for the three months ended 31 March 2018?

Output VAT £ [   ]

LO 6e

61 Branimir is registered for VAT and is preparing his VAT return for the three-month period ended 31 March 2018. During this period he made zero-rated supplies of £23,000 and standard-rated supplies of £29,560. These figures are VAT exclusive.

Branimir incurred input tax related to the zero-rated supplies of £2,130 and input tax related to the standard-rated supplies of £900. Branimir also paid salaries of £5,800 for the three-month period which relate to the business as a whole.

How much input VAT should Branimir account for on his VAT return for the three months ended 31 March 2018?

Input VAT £ [   ]

LO 6e

62 Eloise started in business as a sole trader on 1 January 2017 making only taxable supplies. Her turnover in the first 18 months of trade was as follows.

1 January 2017 to 31 August 2017   £6,150 per month
September and October 2017   £11,500 per month
From November 2017 onwards   £13,000 per month

By what date should Eloise have notified HMRC that she was required to become VAT registered in order to avoid a late registration penalty?

A   1 January 2017
B   30 November 2017
C   30 December 2017
D   30 January 2018

LO 6c

---

63 James is employed by Aqua Ltd. He is provided with a car with CO_2 emissions of 185g/km and petrol for business and private use.

The VAT-inclusive quarterly scale rate for a car with CO_2 emissions between 185g/km and 189g/km is £379.

What is the output VAT due for the quarter to 31 January 2018?

A   379
B   75.80
C   63.17
D   189.50

LO 6d

Chapter 12: Value added tax – further aspects

1   Lavender Ltd has prepared its VAT return for the quarter ended 31 March 2018.

By what date should Lavender Ltd submit its VAT return for the quarter ended 31 March 2018?

A   31 March 2018
B   30 April 2018
C   7 May 2018

By what date should Lavender Ltd pay its VAT relating to the quarter ended 31 March 2018?

D   31 March 2018
E   30 April 2018
F   7 May 2018   LO 2d

2   Cornflower plc had an annual VAT liability in 2017 of £3,000,000. Its VAT liability for the quarter ended 31 March 2018 is £900,000.

Which of the following options correctly identifies Cornflower plc's required VAT payments for the quarter ended 31 March 2018?

A   A single payment of £900,000
B   Three separate payments of £300,000 each
C   Two payments of £250,000 each and a balancing payment of £400,000
D   Two payments of £125,000 each and a balancing payment of £650,000   LO 6f

3   What is the maximum invoice value if a trader wishes to issue a simplified VAT invoice?

A   £50
B   £100
C   £250
D   £1,000   LO 1d

4   Which **two** of the following statements are **not** correct in relation to VAT invoices?

A   A VAT invoice must be issued to all taxable and non-taxable customers.

B   A VAT invoice must contain certain details including the VAT registration number, the total VAT chargeable and a description of the goods supplied.

C   A simplified invoice may be issued if the VAT-inclusive sale proceeds are less than £500.

D   The VAT invoice is the usual record used to support a recovery of input VAT.   LO 1d

5   Dilara has a business with a year ended 31 December 2017. Dilara uses the annual accounting scheme.

Which of the following statements is correct?

A   She pays all of her VAT in one balancing payment and submits her return by 7 February 2018.

B   She pays all of her VAT in one balancing payment and submits her return by 28 February 2018.

C   She pays her VAT in nine monthly instalments starting in April 2017 with a balancing payment and the return submitted by 7 February 2018.

D   She pays her VAT in nine monthly instalments starting in April 2017 with a balancing payment and the return submitted by 28 February 2018.   LO 6f

---

6   Duffey operates the annual accounting scheme for his VAT payments. He opted to make nine monthly payments during the year. His total VAT liability in the year ended 31 March 2017 was £20,000 and in the year ended 31 March 2018 is £22,500.

What is the final balancing payment of his VAT for the year ended 31 March 2018?

A   £2,500 by 7 May 2018
B   £2,500 by 31 May 2018
C   £4,500 by 7 May 2018
D   £4,500 by 31 May 2018   LO 6f

---

7   Michael is registered for VAT. He issues full invoices for goods sold for more than £250, and simplified invoices for goods sold for less than £250.

In relation to which of these invoices, if either, is Michael required to retain copies?

A   Neither
B   Detailed invoices only
C   Simplified invoices only
D   Both   LO 1d

---

8   What is the maximum permitted annual taxable turnover for a trader to join the annual accounting scheme?

A   £100,000
B   £1,350,000
C   £1,600,000
D   £150,000   LO 6f

---

9   Which of the following statements about the VAT payments on account scheme for substantial traders is true?

A   Under the payments on account scheme VAT is paid in quarterly instalments.

B   Under the payments on account scheme VAT is paid in instalments every other month (ie, six payments per annum).

C   Each payment on account is 1/24 of the total VAT liability of the previous year.

D   The balancing amount for the year, if any, is payable two months after the year end.   LO 6f

10   Which **two** of the following statements about VAT are true?

   A   Businesses with taxable turnover greater than £2.3 million must join the VAT payments on account scheme.

   B   Businesses operating the flat rate scheme apply their sector percentage to total (both taxable and exempt) VAT inclusive turnover.

   C   HMRC may grant exemption from registration to zero rated traders that have negligible amounts of input VAT.

   D   Businesses operating the annual accounting scheme must still file VAT returns every quarter.

   E   Businesses operating the cash accounting scheme cannot also join the annual accounting scheme.   LO 6f

11   Which **two** of the following statements concerning cash accounting are **not** true?

   A   VAT is accounted for on the basis of cash paid and received rather than on invoices.

   B   Automatic bad debt relief is received.

   C   The scheme is advantageous for businesses making only zero rated supplies.

   D   The scheme is advantageous for businesses offering extended credit to customers.

   E   Businesses in the scheme must leave if taxable supplies in the previous 12 months exceed £1.35 million.   LO 6f

12   A trader may join the annual accounting scheme where the taxable turnover in the following year is not expected to exceed £ [   ]   LO 6f

13   Major plc had a VAT liability of £3 million in its year ended 31 October 2017. The VAT liability for the quarter to 30 April 2018 is £800,000.

   Assuming the correct payments on account have been made, how much is due by 31 May 2018?

   A   £800,000
   B   £550,000
   C   £300,000
   D   £125,000   LO 6f

14   Which of the following is **not** a feature of the annual accounting scheme?

   A   There is a reduction in the number of VAT returns required
   B   Automatic bad debt relief is given
   C   The VAT return is due two months after the end of the year
   D   Payments on account must be made   LO 6f

15   Which of the following is **not** a feature of the flat rate scheme?

   A   Businesses calculate VAT due as a flat rate percentage of their VAT exclusive turnover
   B   The percentage applied depends on the type of business
   C   Businesses issue normal tax invoices to customers
   D   There is a 1% reduction in the flat rate percentage during the first year of VAT registration   LO 6f

16 Giovanna makes standard-rated supplies. She voluntarily registered for VAT from her first day of trading and simultaneously joined the flat rate scheme. The flat rate percentage she must use is 11%.

She has now been trading for two years. For her latest trading quarter Giovanna had total turnover of £8,500 (exclusive of VAT). Giovanna's total purchases were £2,400 (exclusive of VAT).

How much VAT is payable to HMRC for Giovanna's latest trading quarter?

A £671
B £805
C £935
D £1,122   LO 6f

17 Florence Ltd is a VAT-registered business which operates the cash accounting scheme. During the quarter ended 31 December 2017 it made the following purchases:

	Goods received	Date paid	Input VAT suffered £
Artwork for reception	30 November 2017	15 December 2017	1,150
Spare machinery parts	1 December 2017	13 January 2018	242
Marketing literature	1 September 2017	1 October 2017	858

How much input tax can Florence Ltd recover on these items in the VAT return for the quarter ended 31 December 2017?

A £1,150
B £1,392
C £2,008
D £2,250   LO 6f

18 Gordon, a VAT-registered trader who is a member of the cash accounting scheme, supplies some goods to a customer. The order is received from the customer on 5 May and the goods are despatched on 13 May. An invoice is issued on 16 May and payment is received from the customer on 4 June.

What is the tax point of the supply?

A 5 May
B 13 May
C 16 May
D 4 June   LO 6d/6f

19 Tony has been VAT-registered for many years, making only standard-rated supplies. He is a member of the flat rate scheme for VAT. The flat rate percentage based on his trade sector is 8%.

In the quarter ended 31 March 2018 Tony made sales of £17,000 (exclusive of VAT). Tony's total purchases were £6,400 (exclusive of VAT).

How much VAT is payable to HMRC for the quarter ended 31 March 2018?

A £848
B £1,018
C £1,360
D £1,632   LO 6f

20   Which **two** statements about the flat rate scheme are correct?

    A   A trader can join if he expects total net turnover for the next 12 months not to exceed £150,000.

    B   A trader using the flat rate scheme may also be authorised to use the annual accounting scheme.

    C   The flat rate is applied to the VAT-exclusive turnover.

    D   Where a customer requires an invoice, a flat rate trader who makes wholly standard-rated supplies will issue a VAT invoice showing 20% output tax.   LO 6f

21   Which **two** statements about the cash accounting scheme for VAT are correct?

    A   A VAT return is completed once a year.
    B   Automatic bad debt relief is given.
    C   Output VAT is accounted for when cash is received from the customer.
    D   Output VAT is calculated by applying a flat rate percentage to the VAT inclusive turnover.
    E   VAT is paid over to HMRC each month by direct debit.   LO 6f

22   How does a limited cost trader using the flat rate scheme calculate VAT due?

    A   20% × VAT inclusive turnover.
    B   16.5% of VAT inclusive turnover.
    C   20% × VAT exclusive turnover.
    D   16.5% of VAT exclusive turnover.   LO 6f

Principles of Taxation: Question Bank

Chapter 13: Administration of tax

1   Camilla began trading in January 2017. Camilla's profit for the year ended 31 December 2017 was £56,000. She has not informed HMRC that she has begun to trade and has never been issued with or completed a self-assessment return.

   What is the latest date by which Camilla should have contacted HMRC to obtain a self-assessment return?

   A   5 October 2017
   B   31 October 2017
   C   31 January 2018
   D   5 October 2018   LO 2c

2   Anne received her self assessment return relating to the year 2017/18 on 15 December 2018.

   What is the latest date by which Anne should submit her return online?

   A   31 December 2018
   B   31 January 2019
   C   15 March 2019
   D   31 March 2019   LO 2d

3   Andrew is an employee (not a director) of Toes Ltd with an annual salary of £50,000 and bank interest of approximately £1,500 per year.

   What type of self assessment return is Andrew required to file each year?

   A   Andrew may file a short tax return
   B   Andrew must file a full tax return

   Assuming Andrew were to leave his employment to set up in business with a turnover of £10,000 per annum, what type of self assessment return would he then be required to file each year?

   C   Andrew may file a short tax return
   D   Andrew must file a full tax return   LO 2c

4   Edward is an employee of Theatre Ltd with an annual salary of £66,000. In addition, Edward has run his own business for a number of years with an average annual profit of about £25,000.

   What is the end of the statutory retention period for Edward's records relating to the tax year ended 5 April 2018?

   A   31 January 2023
   B   31 January 2024

   James is an employee of Stage Ltd with an annual salary of £45,000. He also owns a number of shares on which he receives dividend income in excess of £10,000 per year.

   What is the end of the statutory retention period for James's records relating to the tax year ended 5 April 2018?

   C   31 January 2020
   D   31 January 2021   LO 2a

5 Beatrice received her tax return for the tax year 2016/17 in April 2017 and filed it on 31 March 2018. She has now realised that she made a mistake in the return and wishes to amend it accordingly.

What is the latest date by which the amendment can be made?

A   5 April 2019
B   30 April 2019
C   31 January 2019
D   31 March 2019   LO 2c

6 Eugenie is a higher-rate taxpayer. She is an employee and has run her own business as a sole trader with profits in excess of £100,000 per annum for a number of years.

When is Eugenie's income tax not deducted at source payable for the year 2017/18?

A   31 January 2018 and 31 July 2019
B   31 January 2018, 31 July 2018 and 31 January 2019
C   31 July 2018 and 31 January 2019
D   31 January 2019   LO 2d

7 Harry's total income tax liability for 2016/17 was £15,000 and his Class 4 NIC liability was £2,000. During 2016/17 £6,000 of his income tax liability was paid via tax deducted at source. Harry's capital gains tax liability for 2016/17 was £2,500.

What is Harry's first payment on account for 2017/18?

Payment on account   £ [   ]   LO 2d

8 Sophie made the following payments of tax relating to 2017/18.

	£
1st payment on account 15 February 2018	22,000
2nd payment on account 31 August 2018	15,000
Balancing payment 30 April 2019	11,000

Which of the following statements in relation to Sophie's payments is correct?

A   All of the payments were made late and will be liable to a penalty at 5%.

B   All of the payments were made late and will be liable to interest from the due date to the day before payment plus those made more than 30 days late will be liable to a penalty at 5%.

C   All of the payments were made late and will be liable to interest from the due date to the day before payment but only the balancing payment is liable to a penalty at 5%.

D   All of the payments were made late and will be liable to interest from the due date to the day before payment plus a penalty at 5%.   LO 2e

9   Albert began trading as a sole trader on 1 July 2017.

     What is the latest date by which Albert should have contacted HMRC to obtain a self assessment
     return?

     A   30 September 2017
     B   5 October 2017
     C   5 October 2018
     D   31 January 2019   LO 2c

10   Barbara has been trading as a self-employed beautician for many years. She prepares accounts to
     31 December each year.

     She submitted her tax return for 2017/18 on 1 November 2018.

     Until what date must she retain her business records for the year to 31 December 2017?

     A   31 December 2022
     B   31 December 2023
     C   31 January 2023
     D   31 January 2024   LO 2a

11   A notice to make a 2017/18 tax return was issued to Cuthbert on 30 September 2018.

     Which **two** of the following statements correctly identify when Cuthbert must file the return?

     A   By 30 November 2018 if he wants HMRC to calculate his tax.
     B   By 31 October 2018 if he wants HMRC to calculate his tax.
     C   By 31 December 2018 if he wants HMRC to calculate his tax.
     D   By 31 December 2018 if he wants to file online.
     E   By 31 January 2019 if he wants to file online.   LO 2d

12   Elaine submitted her 2017/18 tax return online on 1 December 2018. The return was issued on
     6 May 2018.

     Which **two** of the following statements are correct?

     A   Elaine can amend her tax return on 15 December 2019.

     B   HMRC can correct an arithmetic error in her return on 29 September 2019.

     C   Elaine can make a claim for overpayment relief because there is an error in her return on
          31 December 2021.

     D   HMRC can give notice of an enquiry into her return on 20 December 2019.   LO 2c

13   Fred submitted his 2017/18 tax return on 1 September 2018. HMRC discovered on 1 October
     2019 that Fred did not disclose a source of taxable income. HMRC believes that this was a genuine
     mistake (ie, not careless or deliberate) by Fred and that he did not intend to avoid paying tax on
     the income.

     If HMRC wishes to collect the unpaid tax, it must raise an assessment by 5 April [   ]

     (Enter a year in the format 20XX)   LO 2c

14 Harriet's income tax liability was £28,450 for 2016/17 and £29,750 for 2017/18. Tax deducted at source was £23,400 in 2016/17 and £23,500 in 2017/18.

What payment on account of her 2017/18 tax liability should Harriet have paid on 31 July 2018?

A £0
B £2,475
C £2,525
D £3,125

LO 2d

15 Ivan's tax position for 2017/18 and the previous year is as follows.

	2016/17 £	2017/18 £
Total income tax liability	15,500	17,000
Class 4 NICs	3,200	3,500
Paid under PAYE	3,800	3,900
Payments on account made	13,000	

On 31 January 2018, to avoid interest charges under self assessment, Ivan should have paid tax of

£ [   ]

Ignore Class 2 NIC.

LO 2d

16 John's income tax and capital gains tax liabilities for 2016/17 were £18,200 and £4,200 respectively. He paid £5,000 PAYE and payments on account for 2016/17 of £6,000.

His income tax liability for 2017/18 is £19,500 and his capital gains tax liability is £6,500.

What payment on account of his 2017/18 tax liability should John have paid on 31 July 2018?

A £9,750
B £7,250
C £6,600
D £3,000

LO 2d

17 Kurt had an income tax liability of £9,500 and a capital gains tax liability of £2,300 for 2016/17. The tax payable under self-assessment for 2015/16 was £8,000.

Kurt has made the following payments towards his 2016/17 tax liability.

	Cash paid £
15 February 2017	3,500
29 July 2017	4,500
15 March 2018	3,800
	11,800

What late payment penalties are payable by Kurt relating to his 2016/17 liability?

A £365
B £190
C £380
D £590

LO 2e

18　Martha filed her 2016/17 tax return online on 5 January 2018. On 31 March 2018 HMRC amended the return to show additional tax due of £1,500. Martha paid the tax on 15 May 2018.

Which of the following statements are true?

Interest will run on the additional liability of £1,500 from 1 April 2018 to 14 May 2018.

A　True
B　False

A late payment penalty of £75 is payable by Martha.

C　True
D　False

LO 2e

19　Which of the following statements about the appeals procedure are true?

An appeal against a discovery assessment must be made in writing within a calendar month of the date of the assessment.

A　True
B　False

The taxpayer must first apply for an internal review before making an appeal to the First-tier Tribunal.

C　True
D　False

A taxpayer can appeal against and apply to postpone the tax due under an assessment raised as a result of an enquiry into a tax return.

E　True
F　False

LO 2f

20　Andrea's only source of income is from employment and she does not normally complete a tax return. On 1 May 2017 she sold a painting generating a chargeable gain of £100,000.

By what date is she required to notify HMRC of the chargeable gain?

A　1 May 2018
B　5 October 2018
C　31 October 2018
D　31 January 2019

LO 2c

21　Ethel submitted her 2017/18 tax return on 1 December 2018. She deliberately omitted to include rental income from an overseas property to save tax, as she did not think that HMRC would find out about the income.

Until what date can HMRC raise a discovery assessment to collect tax on the undisclosed income?

A　5 April 2022
B　5 April 2024
C　5 April 2038
D　5 April 2039

LO 2c

22 Fred owes unpaid income tax to HMRC. HMRC is seeking to recover the debt directly from Fred's bank account.

Which **two** of the following statements are correct?

A   HMRC can recover the debt in this way only if exceeds £5,000.
B   Before the debt is recovered, there will be period when Fred can object to the recovery.
C   Fred must be left with at least £1,000 in his accounts after the debt recovery.
D   HMRC must be satisfied that Fred is aware that the sum is due.

LO 2c

23 Greg's tax position for 2017/18 and the previous year is as follows:

	2016/17 £	2017/18 £
Total income tax liability	23,200	24,300
Paid under PAYE	19,000	19,200
Capital gains tax	3,200	1,200

How much tax should Greg have paid on account on 31 July 2018?

A   £0
B   £2,550
C   £2,100
D   £3,700

LO 2d

24 Harold's tax position for 2017/18 and the previous year is as follows.

	2016/17 £	2017/18 £
Total income tax liability	12,100	13,250
Class 4 NIC	3,400	3,550
Tax deducted at source	300	500

As at 30 July 2018 Harold has paid £5,500 on account of his 2017/18 tax liability.

Harold is due to make a payment on 31 July 2018. To minimise any interest charges you would advise that he makes a payment on that date of £ [   ]

LO 2d

25 Ingrid had tax payable under self assessment for 2015/16 of £8,500. She submitted her income tax return for 2016/17 online on 15 February 2018. The return showed an income tax liability of £10,100 and a capital gains tax liability of £1,200. On the same date she paid the outstanding tax of £2,800.

Ingrid had made two equal payments on account totalling £8,500 on 15 January 2017 and 31 August 2017 in respect of 2016/17.

What is the amount of any penalties payable by Ingrid in respect of 2016/17?

A   £0
B   £100
C   £240
D   £2,900

LO 2e

26 A notice to submit a 2017/18 tax return was issued to Laura on 30 November 2018. When must Laura file the return by if

she wants HMRC to calculate her tax liability?

A   28 January 2019
B   31 January 2019
C   28 February 2019

she intends to calculate her own tax liability?

D   28 January 2019
E   31 January 2019
F   28 February 2019   LO 2d

27 Asha received trading income of £60,000 in 2017/18. She also received property income of £700 per month from an investment property she has owned for many years. On 10 September 2018 Asha submitted her self-assessment tax return for 2017/18.

By when must Asha pay the balancing payment of tax due for 2017/18?

A   31 January 2019
B   10 June 2019
C   10 September 2019
D   31 January 2020

By when must HMRC correct any obvious errors in Asha's 2017/18 return?

E   31 January 2019
F   10 June 2019
G   10 September 2019
H   31 January 2020   LO 2c/2d

28 Roof Ltd has yet to pay its PAYE due for the last month of 2016/17. It has also failed to submit its P11D forms relating to 2016/17. Roof Ltd does not make payments electronically.

What is the due date for payment of the PAYE relating to the final month of 2016/17?

A   14 April 2017
B   19 April 2017

What is the due date for the submission of P11D forms relating to 2016/17?

C   31 May 2017
D   6 July 2017   LO 2d

29 Which of the following correctly identifies a P45 form?

A   End of year form recording details of benefits provided to employees
B   Form issued when an employee leaves employment

Select which of the following correctly identifies a P60 form.

C   End of year summary of tax and NICs for all employees for submission to HMRC
D   End of year summary of tax and NICs per employee to be issued to each employee   LO 2b

30 What is the maximum penalty for filing an incorrect P11D form, where the error was not deliberate?

A   30% potential lost revenue
B   70% potential lost revenue

What is the maximum initial penalty for the late filing of a P11D form?

C   £300 per return
D   £3,000 per return   LO 2e

31 By which date must an employer provide a completed Form P60 to an employee?

A   6 July
B   31 May
C   19 May
D   30 April   LO 2d

32 Soap Ltd employs 30 people in the manufacture of bathroom products. Remuneration packages offered to employees include company cars and private medical insurance in addition to a basic salary and bonuses.

By what date must Soap Ltd submit each of the following PAYE returns for 2017/18 to its employees or HMRC.

Form P11D

A   6 July 2018
B   19 July 2018

Form P60

C   19 May 2018
D   31 May 2018   LO 2d

33 Abacus plc filed its corporation tax return for the year ended 31 December 2016 on time. It has now realised that an error was made and it wishes to rectify this via a claim for 'overpayment relief' as it will otherwise result in an overpayment of tax.

What is the latest date by which the claim must be made?

A   31 December 2017
B   31 December 2018
C   31 December 2020
D   31 December 2022   LO 2c

34 Indigo plc filed its corporation tax return for the year ended 31 December 2016 on 30 November 2017. HMRC wishes to correct some obvious errors in the return.

What is the latest date by which HMRC may make such corrections?

A   31 August 2018
B   30 September 2018
C   30 November 2018
D   31 December 2018   LO 2c

35   Azure plc filed its corporation tax return for the year ended 31 December 2016 on 28 February
      2018. HMRC wishes to conduct an enquiry into the corporation tax return.

      What is the latest date by which HMRC may give notice of its intention to enquire?

      A   31 December 2018
      B   28 February 2019
      C   31 March 2019
      D   30 April 2019   LO 2f

36   Ebony plc submitted its corporation tax return for its year ended 31 August 2016 on 1 July 2018.
      Ebony plc paid the corporation tax liability relating to this return on 1 April 2018. Ebony plc has
      submitted previous corporation tax returns on time.

      What is the fixed penalty for failing to file its corporation tax return on time?

      A   £100
      B   £200

      What is the tax-geared penalty for failing to file its corporation tax return on time?

      C   10% of tax unpaid at 28 February 2018
      D   20% of tax unpaid at 28 February 2018   LO 2e

37   Pilot Ltd prepares accounts to 30 April each year.

Year end	Corporation tax due	Date return filed	Date tax paid
30 April 2016	£35,000	12 October 2017	15 December 2017

      Pilot Ltd also submitted its two previous corporation tax returns late.

      What is Pilot Ltd's liability to penalties for the late filing of its corporation tax return for the year
      ended 30 April 2016?

      A   £200 fixed penalty and no tax-geared penalty
      B   £200 fixed penalty and 10% tax-geared penalty
      C   £1,000 fixed penalty and no tax-geared penalty
      D   £1,000 fixed penalty and 10% tax-geared penalty   LO 2e

38   Blunt Ltd manufactures stationery and has prepared its corporation tax return for the year ended
      31 March 2018.

      Jim is a sole trader. He has been a retailer of stationery for many years and has just finished
      preparing his accounts to 31 December 2017.

      What is the latest date for which Blunt Ltd and Jim must keep their business records for tax
      purposes?

      Blunt Ltd

      A   31 March 2019
      B   31 March 2023
      C   31 March 2024

      Jim

      D   31 January 2019
      E   31 January 2024
      F   31 January 2025   LO 2a

39 Edmund is a trader whose taxable supplies exceeded the VAT-registration threshold 10 months ago. His friend explains to him that he should have registered for VAT. Edmund registers and pays the outstanding tax immediately.

What is the minimum penalty HMRC could impose for Edmund's late registration?

A   30% of potential lost revenue
B   20% of potential lost revenue
C   10% of potential lost revenue
D   £0   LO 2e

40 Which **two** of the following statements are correct?

A   Amy's VAT return for the quarter to 28 February 2018 should have been submitted by 30 March 2018.

B   Bob & Charles' partnership income tax return for 2017/18 received on 3 November 2018 should be submitted online by 31 January 2019.

C   Daniel's full income tax return for 2017/18 received on 4 July 2018 should be submitted to HMRC by 31 October 2018, if Daniel wants HMRC to calculate the tax.

D   Eagle Ltd's corporation tax return for the year ended 31 December 2017 should be submitted by 1 October 2018.

E   Frank Ltd's P11Ds for 2017/18 should be submitted to HMRC by 6 July 2018.   LO 2d

41 Talia submitted her VAT return for the quarter to 31 December 2017 online on 16 February 2018 and paid the VAT due of £10,000 on that day. She had paid VAT late in respect of the previous two quarters but had otherwise paid VAT and filed VAT returns on time.

Talia's default surcharge for the return for the quarter to 31 December 2017 is

A   £0
B   £200
C   £500
D   £1,000   LO 2e

42 Rand submitted his VAT return for the quarter to 31 October 2017 online on 15 December 2017 and paid the VAT due of £5,000 on that day. The only other time that he has ever submitted a VAT return late was in his quarter to 30 April 2017.

HMRC is likely to impose a default surcharge for the return for the quarter to 31 October 2017 on Rand of

A   £0
B   £100
C   £250
D   £400   LO 2e

43 Karli set up her business on 1 January 2016. Due to the amount of work she undertook she should have been VAT registered from 30 June 2017 but she did not notify HMRC until 16 November 2018. The unpaid VAT between 30 June 2017 and 16 November 2018 was £10,800. HMRC does not consider being too busy a reasonable excuse for failure to register on time.

The minimum penalty payable by Karli (assuming HMRC deems the failure to notify not to be deliberate) for late registration is

A   £0
B   £1,080
C   £2,160
D   £3,240

LO 2e

44 John, a sole trader, completed a VAT return for the quarter to 31 December 2016 showing output tax of £120,000 and input tax of £70,000.

In June 2017 John's accountant discovered that the input tax on the VAT return had been overstated by £45,000. This was the first error that John had made on his VAT returns. HMRC was notified and the outstanding tax paid.

Which of the following correctly describes the error?

A   Careless
B   Deliberate but not concealed
C   Deliberate and concealed

What is the minimum penalty HMRC could charge John for the error?

D   30% of potential lost revenue
E   15% of potential lost revenue
F   0% of potential lost revenue

LO 2e

45 Glitch plc's VAT returns have always been accurate, but the return to 31 December 2017 contains an error. Turnover is correctly stated at £5.6 million, but input tax is overstated by £52,700.

Which of the following statements is correct?

A   A correction can be made in the next VAT return because the error is less than 1% of turnover.

B   A correction cannot be made in the next VAT return because the error exceeds £2,000.

C   A correction cannot be made in the next VAT return because the error exceeds £10,000.

D   A correction cannot be made in the next VAT return because the error exceeds £50,000.

LO 6e

46 Ethel submitted her 2017/18 tax return on 1 December 2018. She did not include rental income of £15,000 as she did not think that HMRC would find out about the income. Ethel is a higher-rate taxpayer.

HMRC conducts an enquiry into Ethel's return and in reply Ethel makes a disclosure of the rental income.

What is the minimum penalty that could be charged by HMRC on Ethel for her error?

A   £6,000
B   £4,200
C   £2,100
D   £1,200

LO 2e

47 Which of the following would definitely **not** constitute a reasonable excuse for late filing of a return?

A   Serious illness leading up to the filing date
B   Postal disruption
C   Failure of a taxpayer's IT systems close to the filing date
D   Insufficient funds to pay the tax due

LO 2e

48 Shed Ltd has failed to pay its PAYE due of £4,600 for the month ended 5 February 2018 on time. Payment was made on 17 March 2018. It had also failed to pay PAYE on time on two other occasions during 2017/18.

What is the amount of any penalty payable by Shed Ltd for late payment of PAYE for the month ended 5 February 2018?

A   £92
B   £0
C   £138
D   £46

LO 2e

49 A taxpayer may be able to appeal against an information notice.

A   True
B   False

A taxpayer may be able to appeal against an inspection notice.

C   True
D   False

LO 2e

50 An employer can use voluntary payrolling to report all benefits.

A   True
B   False

An employer can use voluntary payrolling to report company car benefits.

C   True
D   False

An employer can use voluntary payrolling to report employer provided living accommodation benefits.

E   True
F   False

LO 2b

1   During 2017/18, Mildred received interest income of £100 on a loan she had made to her friend, Dot.

Mildred has been employed part-time by ABC Ltd since 2008. She received the following remuneration package in 2017/18:

- salary £15,000 per year;
- free meals offered to all staff in the work canteen, which cost the company £560 for Mildred;
- childcare vouchers of £45 per week (ie, £2,340 pa) which have been provided since 2008; and
- use of a diesel company car since 1 July 2017 with CO_2 emissions of 130g/km. ABC Ltd paid £16,000 for the car although it has a list price of £18,000. Mildred pays for all her private fuel.

Mildred received £18,900 of dividends in January 2018 from a UK company.

Mildred has also run her own business as a sole trader for many years. Mildred has calculated her taxable trading profits for 2017/18 to be £30,700. In arriving at her taxable trading profits, Mildred deducted the following amounts:

- £2,000 for legal and professional fees relating to the acquisition of a new five-year lease of business premises;
- £170 accountancy fees for preparation of annual accounts;
- Mildred's class 2 national insurance liability of £148; and
- £150 of irrecoverable VAT relating to the purchase of stock for which Mildred has lost the VAT invoice.

Requirement

Using the standard format below, compute Mildred's taxable income for 2017/18. You should enter a number in each relevant box. If an amount is not taxable enter a zero or a dash into the relevant box.

	Non-savings income £	Savings income £	Dividend income £
Trading Income (W1)			
Employment income (W2)			
Interest from loan to Dot			
Dividends			
Net income			
Personal allowance			
Taxable income			

W1 – Trading income

	£
Trading profits	
Legal & professional fees	
Accountancy fees	
Class 2 NIC	
VAT re stock purchase	
Tax-adjusted trading profits	

W2 – Employment income

	£
Salary	
Free meals	
Childcare vouchers	
Car	
Total employment income	

LOs 3a, 3c, 3e, 3j

2 Elan received £100 interest income from a building society ISA during 2017/18.

Elan has been employed part-time by DEF Ltd for many years. He received the following remuneration package in 2017/18:

- salary £21,000 per year;

- a bonus of £1,250 in respect of the year ended 31 March 2017, paid on 31 May 2017;

- mobile phone, costing DEF Ltd £240 per annum; and

- use of a petrol company car with CO_2 emissions of 132g/km, and a list price of £20,000. The company also paid for all of Elan's private fuel.

Elan received £112,000 of dividends in January 2018 from a UK company.

Elan has also run his own business as a sole trader for many years. Elan has calculated his taxable trading profits for 2017/18 to be £44,100. In arriving at his taxable trading profits, Elan deducted the following amounts:

- £1,200 written off as a bad debt because a customer has gone into liquidation;

- £50 parking fines incurred by an employee while visiting a customer;

- £600 in respect of entertaining clients at a summer party; and

- £50 paid to a local charity for which Elan received an advertisement for his business in the charity's newsletter.

Requirement

Using the standard format below, compute Elan's taxable income for 2017/18. You should enter a number in each relevant box. If an amount is not taxable enter a zero or a dash into the relevant box.

	Non-savings income £	Savings income £	Dividend income £
Trading Income (W1)			
Employment income (W2)			
ISA interest			
Dividends			
Net income			
Personal allowance			
Taxable income			

W1 – Trading income

	£
Trading profits	
Bad debt written off	
Parking fine	
Entertaining	
Donation to charity	
Tax-adjusted trading profits	

W2 – Employment income

	£
Salary	
Bonus	
Mobile phone	
Car	
Total employment income	

LOs 3a, 3c, 3e, 3j

3   Becky received £175 of bank interest income during 2017/18.

Becky has been employed part-time by GHI Ltd for several years. She received the following remuneration package in 2017/18:

- salary £16,000 per year;

- pension advice, costing £125 in respect of Becky, and offered to all employees;

- use of a bicycle which cost GHI Ltd £280 for business and private journeys, as provided to all employees; and

- provision of a house owned by GHI Ltd, with an annual value of £12,000. The house cost the company £200,000 in 2013. The official rate of interest on 6 April 2017 was 2.5%.

Becky received £7,500 of dividends in December 2017 from an overseas company.

Becky has also run her own business as a sole trader for many years. Becky has calculated her draft taxable trading profits for 2017/18 to be £19,000. In arriving at her draft taxable trading profits, no account has been taken of the following amounts as Becky was unsure of the correct treatment:

- £20 parking fine incurred by Becky when visiting a client;

- £80 Gift Aid donation to a national charity;

- overdraft interest of £160 on Becky's business bank account; and

- professional fees of £300 incurred in collecting debts from customers who were slow in paying.

Requirement

Using the standard format below, compute Becky's taxable income for 2017/18. You should enter a number in each relevant box. If an amount is not taxable enter a zero or a dash into the relevant box.

	Non-savings income £	Savings income £	Dividend income £
Trading Income (W1)			
Employment income (W2)			
Bank interest			
Dividends			
Net income			
Personal allowance			
Taxable income			

W1 – Trading income

	£
Trading profits	
Fine	
Donation	
Overdraft interest	
Professional fees	
Tax-adjusted trading profits	

W2 – Employment income

	£
Salary	
Pension advice	
Bicycle	
Accommodation	
Total employment income	

LOs 3a, 3c, 3e, 3j

4   During 2017/18, Mandy received interest of £120 from a National Savings and Investments Direct Saver account.

Mandy has been employed part-time by JKL Ltd since 2008. She received the following remuneration package in 2017/18:

- salary £25,000 per year;

- gift of a painting from a client worth £60;

- eye test, costing £20, offered to all employees who use VDU equipment; and

- from 1 October 2017, use of a van for 20% work, 80% private use, with CO_2 emissions of 150g/km. The van had a list price of £9,000 and JKL Ltd paid for all Mandy's private fuel.

Mandy received £9,000 of dividends in March 2018 from an ISA.

Mandy has also run her own business as a sole trader for many years. Mandy has calculated her taxable trading profits for 2017/18 to be £34,000. In arriving at her taxable trading profits, Mandy deducted the following amounts:

- £300 for the cost of gifts of a bottle of wine (£20 per bottle) to 15 clients;
- £375 for redecorating the office;
- a donation to a UK political party of £250; and
- legal fees of £800 for the review of employment contracts.

Requirement

Using the standard format below, compute Mandy's taxable income for 2017/18. You should enter a number in each relevant box. If an amount is not taxable enter a zero or a dash into the relevant box.

	Non-savings income £	Savings income £	Dividend income £
Trading Income (W1)			
Employment income (W2)			
Direct Saver interest			
Dividends			
Net income			
Personal allowance			
Taxable income			

W1 – Trading income

	£
Trading profits	
Gifts	
Redecorating	
Donation	
Legal fees	
Tax-adjusted trading profits	

W2 – Employment income

	£
Salary	
Gift from client	
Eye test	
Van	
Total employment income	

LOs 3a, 3c, 3e, 3j

5   Jorge received £500 of premium bond winnings during 2017/18.

Jorge has been employed part-time by MNO Ltd since 2013. He received the following remuneration package in 2017/18:

- salary £45,000 per year;
- private medical insurance, costing MNO Ltd £500;
- a parking space at the office of MNO Ltd, which saved Jorge £500 pa; and
- childcare vouchers of £50 per week (ie, £2,600 pa).

Jorge received £950 of dividends in June 2017 from a UK company.

Jorge has also run his own business as a sole trader for many years. Jorge has calculated his draft taxable trading profits for 2017/18 to be £112,000. In arriving at his draft taxable trading profits, no account has been taken of the following costs as Jorge was unsure of the correct treatment:

- £800 for a staff party for two employees;
- £2,000 for stock donated to a local school;
- £5,000 on salary for himself; and
- £1,500 written off on a loan to a former employee.

Requirement

Using the standard format below, compute Jorge's taxable income for 2017/18. You should enter a number in each relevant box. If an amount is not taxable enter a zero or a dash into the relevant box.

	Non-savings income £	Savings income £	Dividend income £
Trading Income (W1)			
Employment income (W2)			
Premium bond winnings			
Dividends			
Net income			
Personal allowance			
Taxable income			

W1 – Trading income

	£
Trading profits	
Staff party	
Stock donation	
Salary	
Loan write off	
Tax-adjusted trading profits	

W2 – Employment income

	£
Salary	
Private medical insurance	
Parking space	
Childcare vouchers	
Total employment income	

LOs 3a, 3c, 3e, 3j

6   Sandra received bank interest income of £100 during 2017/18.

Sandra has been employed part-time by PQR Ltd, which operates a cookery school, since 2010. She received the following remuneration package in 2017/18:

- salary £20,000 per year;

- attendance at a health and safety annual course for people working with catering equipment, costing the company £80;

- assets for private use being a television with a market value of £825 when first provided in 2015, and a mobile phone with contract costs for 2017/18 of £150; and

- free cookery classes for her son. A member of the public would have paid £500 to attend the classes. PQR Ltd spent an extra £100 on ingredients for Sandra's son to attend.

Sandra received £540 of dividends in February 2018 from a UK company.

Sandra has also run her own business as a sole trader for many years. Sandra has calculated her taxable trading profits for 2017/18 to be £28,400. In arriving at her taxable trading profits, Sandra deducted the following amounts:

- £1,600, which was the cost of leasing, for business use only, a new car with CO_2 emissions of 150g/km from 1 May 2017 until the end of 2017/18;

- employer's national insurance contributions of £567, paid in respect of Sandra's employee;

- legal fees of £1,000 in respect of the renewal of a five-year lease over an industrial unit Sandra uses for her business; and

- £150 for depreciation of office equipment used for Sandra's business.

Requirement

Using the standard format below, compute Sandra's taxable income for 2017/18. You should enter a number in each relevant box. If an amount is not taxable enter a zero or a dash into the relevant box.

	Non-savings income £	Savings income £	Dividend income £
Trading Income (W1)			
Employment income (W2)			
Bank interest			
Dividends			
Net income			
Personal allowance			
Taxable income			

W1 – Trading income

	£
Trading profits	
Car lease	
Employer's NIC	
Legal fees	
Depreciation	
Tax-adjusted trading profits	

W2 – Employment income

	£
Salary	
Health and safety course	
Assets for private use	
Cookery classes	
Total employment income	

LOs 3a, 3c, 3e, 3j

7   During 2017/18, Leanne received interest income of £60 on a National Savings and Investments investment account.

Leanne has been employed part-time by STU Ltd for many years. She received the following remuneration package in 2017/18:

- salary £18,500 per year;

- pension contribution by the company of £925;

- from 1 October 2017, use of a diesel car with CO_2 emissions of 72g/km. STU Ltd paid £20,000 for the car although it has a list price of £23,000. Leanne pays for all her private fuel; and

- a medical check-up with a private doctor which cost the company £500 and would have cost Leanne £600 is she had paid for it herself.

Leanne received £500 of dividends in March 2018 from a UK company.

Leanne has also run her own business as a sole trader for many years. Leanne has calculated draft her taxable trading profits for 2017/18 to be £19,500. In arriving at her draft taxable trading profits, no account has been taken of the following amounts as Leanne was unsure of the correct treatment:

- £6,000 for building work to extend the office in which Leanne works;

- £230 interest payable on loan to extend office;

- accountancy fees of £500 for payroll services; and

- £100 of irrecoverable VAT relating to the cost of advertising in the local newspaper for which Leanne has lost the VAT invoice.

Requirement

Using the standard format below, compute Leanne's taxable income for 2017/18. You should enter a number in each relevant box. If an amount is not taxable enter a zero or a dash into the relevant box.

	Non-savings income £	Savings income £	Dividend income £
Trading Income (W1)			
Employment income (W2)			
Investment account			
Dividends			
Net income			
Personal allowance			
Taxable income			

W1 – Trading income

	£
Trading profits	
Building work	
Interest	
Accountancy fees	
VAT re advertising	
Tax-adjusted trading profits	

W2 – Employment income

	£
Salary	
Pension contribution	
Car	
Medical	
Total employment income	

LOs 3a, 3c, 3e, 3j

8   During 2017/18, Simon received £15 of income tax repayment interest, which related to overpaid income tax from 2015/16.

Simon has been employed part-time by VWX Ltd for many years. He received the following remuneration package in 2017/18:

- salary £10,000 per year;

- bonus of £200 in respect of the year ended 30 June 2017, paid on 31 July 2017.

- vouchers for a supermarket which can be used to buy £1,000 of goods, and which cost VWX Ltd £950; and

- private use of a camera from 1 July 2017, when the company acquired it for £1,500. Simon paid £90 during 2017/18 towards the use of the camera.

Simon received £1,000 of dividends in May 2017 from an overseas company.

Simon has also run his own business as a sole trader for many years. Simon has calculated his taxable trading profits for 2017/18 to be £29,600. In arriving at his taxable trading profits, Simon deducted the following amounts:

- costs of redecorating his office of £500;
- £2,000 fine for breach of Health and Safety regulations;
- £1,500 being a contribution to his personal pension scheme; and
- £200 fee to arrange an overdraft on his personal bank account to pay for materials.

Requirement

Using the standard format below, compute Simon's taxable income for 2017/18. You should enter a number in each relevant box. If an amount is not taxable enter a zero or a dash into the relevant box.

	Non-savings income £	Savings income £	Dividend income £
Trading Income (W1)			
Employment income (W2)			
Repayment interest			
Dividends			
Net income			
Personal allowance			
Taxable income			

W1 – Trading income

	£
Trading profits	
Decorating	
Fine	
Pension contribution	
Overdraft fee	
Tax-adjusted trading profits	

W2 – Employment income

	£
Salary	
Bonus	
Vouchers	
Camera	
Total employment income	

LOs 3a, 3c, 3e, 3j

9   Finlay received £300 of interest on Treasury stock during 2017/18.

Finlay has been employed part-time by YZZ Ltd since 2010. He received the following remuneration package in 2017/18:

- salary £15,000 per year;

- meal vouchers of £4 per day for 240 days;

- from 1 January 2018, provision of living accommodation, a flat, which was rented by the company for £12,000 pa. The annual value of the flat was £13,000 and market value was £200,000. Finlay paid £300 to the company for use of the flat in 2017/18; and

- attendance at the summer party for staff, which cost YZZ Ltd £120 per employee.

Finlay received £810 of dividends in March 2018 from an ISA.

Finlay has also run his own business as a sole trader for many years. Finlay has calculated his draft taxable trading profits for 2017/18 to be £50,000. In arriving at his draft taxable trading profits, no account has been taken of the following amounts as Finlay was unsure of the correct treatment:

- £2,100 for a contribution into an occupational pension scheme for Finlay's employee;

- £1,700 on registering a patent to use in Finlay's business;

- £1,000 on customer gifts of diaries, costing £10 each and bearing the name of Finlay's business; and

- £190 subscription to the local Chamber of Commerce.

Requirement

Using the standard format below, compute Finlay's taxable income for 2017/18. You should enter a number in each relevant box. If an amount is not taxable enter a zero or a dash into the relevant box.

	Non-savings income £	Savings income £	Dividend income £
Trading Income (W1)			
Employment income (W2)			
Treasury stock interest			
Dividends			
Net income			
Personal allowance			
Taxable income			

W1 – Trading income

	£
Trading profits	
Pension contribution	
Patent	
Diaries	
Subscription	
Tax-adjusted trading profits	

W2 – Employment income

	£
Salary	
Meal vouchers	
Accommodation	
Summer party	
Total employment income	

LOs 3a, 3c, 3e, 3j

10   Victoria received lottery winnings of £17,000 during 2017/18.

Victoria has been employed part-time by ABC Ltd since 2012. She received the following remuneration package in 2017/18:

- salary £123,400 per year;

- attendance at a football match with a client, with ticket costing £60 paid by the client;

- use of childcare facilities at her place of work, costing ABC Ltd £5,000 in respect of Victoria's daughter; and

- use of a company car with CO_2 emissions of 100g/km. The list price was £35,000, and ABC Ltd paid a further £500 in February 2017 on accessories for the car. When originally provided to Victoria in January 2016, Victoria paid £4,000 towards the car's purchase. Victoria pays for all her private fuel.

Victoria received £5,000 of dividends in January 2018 from a UK company.

Victoria has also run her own business as a sole trader for many years. Victoria has calculated her taxable trading profits for 2017/18 to be £19,000. In arriving at her taxable trading profits, Victoria deducted the following amounts:

- £1,000 Gift Aid donation to a national charity;

- £800 repairs to the roof of her office building;

- £1,500 legal fees in relation to a new lease over a storage unit; and

- £900 for the purchase of goods which Victoria then took from the business for her own use, without recording the withdrawal. The goods could have been sold for £1,200.

Requirement

Using the standard format below, compute Victoria's taxable income for 2017/18. You should enter a number in each relevant box. If an amount is not taxable enter a zero or a dash into the relevant box.

	Non-savings income £	Savings income £	Dividend income £
Trading Income (W1)			
Employment income (W2)			
Lottery winnings			
Dividends			
Net income			
Personal allowance			
Taxable income			

W1 – Trading income

	£
Trading profits	
Donation	
Repairs	
Legal fees	
Goods	
Tax-adjusted trading profits	

W2 – Employment income

	£
Salary	
Football match	
Childcare	
Car	
Total employment income	

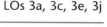 LOs 3a, 3c, 3e, 3j

Scenario-based questions: corporation tax

1a Kennedy Ltd, an unquoted trading company, prepares accounts to 31 December and has no related 51% group companies. The draft accounting profits for the year ended 31 December 2017 are £1,595,000. The following items have been added or deducted in arriving at the draft accounting profit:

	Note	£
Depreciation		202,400
Loan interest payable	1	1,000
Qualifying donation	2	6,000
Exempt dividends received	3	18,000
Bank interest receivable		3,000

Notes:

(1) Interest payable on a loan to buy an investment property.

(2) The qualifying donation of £6,000 in the accounts comprises £3,800 paid during the accounting period and an accrual of £2,200 that the company had agreed to pay but was not paid until 10 January 2018.

(3) Exempt dividends received from unrelated UK companies.

In addition, the following items have not yet been included in the accounts:

- Car leasing charges of £4,200 were incurred for a car used by the managing director. The car has emissions of 165g/km and is used 20% for private purposes.

- The company purchased computer equipment during the year ended 31 December 2017 costing £110,000. The tax written down value on the main pool at 1 January 2017 was £0.

Requirement

Using the standard format below, compute Kennedy Ltd's taxable total profits for the year ended 31 December 2017. You should enter a number in each relevant box. If an amount is not taxable or no adjustment is required you must enter a zero or a dash into the relevant box.

	£
Trading income (W1)	
Non-trading loans	
Dividends	
Qualifying donation	
Taxable total profits	

W1 – Trading income

	£
Draft accounting profits	
Depreciation	
Loan interest payable	
Qualifying donation	
Exempt dividends received	
Bank interest receivable	
Car leasing charges	
Capital allowances	
Trading income	

1b In the year ended 31 December 2018 Kennedy Ltd expects taxable total profits of £1,490,000 and is expected to receive exempt dividends of £20,000 from unrelated UK companies and £5,000 of exempt dividends from an unrelated French company.

Requirement

Complete all the boxes below and state the first date by which any corporation tax should be paid in relation to the year ended 31 December 2018. Input the date in the format DD/MM/YYYY (eg, 03/04/2018 for 3 April 2018).

	£
Taxable total profits	
Exempt ABGH distributions	
Augmented profits	
Corporation tax due date	

LOs 5b, 5c, 5d

2a Sigil Ltd, an unquoted trading company, prepares accounts to 31 March and has no related 51% group companies. The draft accounting profits for the year ended 31 March 2018 are £125,000. The following items have been added or deducted in arriving at the draft accounting profit:

	Note	£
Depreciation		6,300
Loan interest payable	1	2,000
Profit on disposal of asset	2	12,000
Exempt dividends received	3	4,000
Bank interest receivable		5,000
Employee loan interest	4	600

Notes:

(1) Interest payable on a loan to buy a small shareholding in an unrelated company.

(2) Sigil Ltd sold an asset realising a profit on disposal of £12,000. The chargeable gain arising is £9,000.

(3) Exempt dividends of £3,000 received from unrelated UK companies and £1,000 received from unrelated German companies.

(4) Interest of £600 was received on a loan made to an employee in respect of the nine months from 1 April 2017 to 31 December 2017. The employee owed a further £200 in interest as at 31 March 2018.

In addition, the following item has not yet been included in the accounts:

*   The company purchased a car for £20,000 on 1 July 2017 for use by the managing director. The car has emissions of 125g/km and is used 30% for private purposes. The company has not previously owned any plant or cars.

Requirement

Using the standard format below, compute Sigil Ltd's taxable total profits for the year ended 31 March 2018. You should enter a number in each relevant box. If an amount is not taxable or no adjustment is required you must enter a zero or a dash into the relevant box.

	£
Trading income (W1)	
Non-trading loans	
Dividends	
Chargeable gain	
Taxable total profits	

W1 – Trading income

	£
Draft accounting profits	
Depreciation	
Loan interest payable	
Profit on disposal of asset	
Exempt dividends received	
Bank interest receivable	
Employee loan interest	
Capital allowances	
Trading income	

2b In the year ended 31 March 2019 Sigil Ltd expects taxable total profits of £213,000 and is expected to receive the same amount of dividends as in the year ended 31 March 2018.

Requirement

Complete all the boxes below and state the first date by which any corporation tax should be paid in relation to the year ended 31 March 2019. Input the date in the format DD/MM/YYYY (eg, 03/04/2018 for 3 April 2018).

	£
Taxable total profits	
Exempt ABGH distributions	
Augmented profits	

Corporation tax due date	

LOs 5b, 5c, 5d

3a Bryn Ltd, an unquoted trading company, prepares accounts to 30 September and has one related 51% group company. The draft accounting profits for the year ended 30 September 2017 are £890,000. The following items have been added or deducted in arriving at the draft accounting profit:

	Note	£
Depreciation		45,500
Loan interest payable	1	9,000
Qualifying donation	2	8,000
Exempt dividends received	3	27,000
Bank interest receivable		4,200

Notes:

(1) Interest payable on a loan to service working capital.

(2) The qualifying donation of £8,000 in the accounts comprises £1,600 paid during the accounting period and an accrual of £6,400 that the company had agreed to pay but was not paid until 22 December 2017.

(3) Exempt dividends received from unrelated UK companies.

In addition, the following items have not yet been included in the accounts:

• Gifts of one bottle of wine costing £10 to each of 30 employees and each of 22 clients.

• The company purchased a new car for £30,000 with emissions of 65g/km for use by the sales director with 40% private use. The tax written down value on the main pool at 1 October 2016 was £0.

Requirement

Using the standard format below, compute Bryn Ltd's taxable total profits for the year ended 30 September 2017. You should enter a number in each relevant box. If an amount is not taxable or no adjustment is required you must enter a zero or a dash into the relevant box.

	£
Trading income (W1)	
Non-trading loans	
Dividends	
Qualifying donation	
Taxable total profits	

W1 – Trading income

	£
Draft accounting profits	
Depreciation	
Loan interest payable	
Qualifying donation	
Exempt dividends received	
Bank interest receivable	
Gifts	
Capital allowances	
Trading income	

3b   In the year ended 30 September 2018 Bryn Ltd expects taxable total profits of £980,900 and is expected to receive exempt dividends of £40,000 from unrelated UK companies and £10,000 from an unrelated Spanish company.

Requirement

Complete all the boxes below and state the first date by which any corporation tax should be paid in relation to the year ended 30 September 2018. Input the date in the format DD/MM/YYYY (eg, 03/04/2018 for 3 April 2018).

	£
Taxable total profits	
Exempt ABGH distributions	
Augmented profits	

Corporation tax due date	

LOs 5b, 5c, 5d

4a   Lundy Ltd, an unquoted trading company, prepares accounts to 31 March and has no related 51% group companies. The draft accounting profits for the year ended 31 March 2018 are £2,860,000. The following items have been added or deducted in arriving at the draft accounting profit:

	Note	£
Depreciation		148,700
Loan interest payable	1	3,800
Property income	2	25,000
Exempt dividends received	3	9,000
Bank interest receivable		7,000

Notes:

(1)   Interest payable on a loan to buy an investment property.

(2)   Property income relates to an investment property which was rented out to an unrelated company from 1 October 2017 for £5,000 per month payable in advance. The tenant paid the rent for March 2018 late on 8 April 2018.

(3) Exempt dividends of £6,000 received from unrelated UK companies and £3,000 received from an unrelated Italian company.

In addition, the following items have not yet been included in the accounts:

- During the accounting period, legal fees of £4,300 were incurred, of which £4,000 related to the investment property purchase and £300 related to debt collection in respect of trade customers.

- The company purchased a pool car with emissions of 115 g/km during the year ended 31 March 2018 costing £40,000. The tax written down value on the main pool at 1 April 2017 was £0.

Requirement

Using the standard format below, compute Lundy Ltd's taxable total profits for the year ended 31 March 2018. You should enter a number in each relevant box. If an amount is not taxable or no adjustment is required you must enter a zero or a dash into the relevant box.

£

Trading income (W1)	
Non-trading loans	
Dividends	
Property income	
Taxable total profits	

W1 – Trading income

£

Draft accounting profits	
Depreciation	
Loan interest payable	
Property income	
Exempt dividends received	
Bank interest receivable	
Legal fees	
Capital allowances	
Trading income	

4b   In the year ended 31 March 2019 Lundy Ltd expects taxable total profits of £3,100,000 and is expected to receive the same amount of dividends as in the year ended 31 March 2018.

Requirement

Complete all the boxes below and state the first date by which any corporation tax should be paid in relation to the year ended 31 March 2019. Input the date in the format DD/MM/YYYY (eg, 03/04/2018 for 3 April 2018).

£

Taxable total profits	
Exempt ABGH distributions	
Augmented profits	

Corporation tax due date	

LOs 5b, 5c, 5d

5a Knight Ltd, an unquoted trading company, prepares accounts to 31 December and has one wholly owned subsidiary, Sword Ltd. The draft accounting profits for the year ended 31 December 2017 are £467,000. The following items have been added or deducted in arriving at the draft accounting profit:

	Note	£
Depreciation		32,500
Loan interest payable	1	6,400
Property income	2	40,000
Exempt dividends received	3	4,500
Bank interest receivable		5,100
Marketing fees	4	2,000

Notes:

(1) Interest payable on a loan to buy factory premises.

(2) Property income relates to renting out (for £40,000 pa) spare space in Knight Ltd's office building to an unrelated company throughout the accounting period. However, the tenant has left without paying rent for the period from 1 October 2017 to 31 December 2017 and Knight Ltd is unable to recover this.

(3) Exempt dividends received from Sword Ltd, Knight Ltd's wholly-owned subsidiary.

(4) Marketing fees of £2,000 related to advertising one of the company's products online (£1,200) and entertaining prospective customers (£800).

In addition, the following item has not yet been included in the accounts:

• The company purchased 10 vans during the year ended 31 December 2017 costing £80,000 in total. The vans had emissions of 100g/km. The tax written down value on the main pool at 1 January 2017 was £0.

Requirement

Using the standard format below, compute Knight Ltd's taxable total profits for the year ended 31 December 2017. You should enter a number in each relevant box. If an amount is not taxable or no adjustment is required you must enter a zero or a dash into the relevant box.

	£
Trading income (W1)	
Non-trading loans	
Dividends	
Property income	
Taxable total profits	

W1 – Trading income

	£
Draft accounting profits	
Depreciation	
Loan interest payable	
Property income	
Exempt dividends received	
Bank interest receivable	
Marketing fees	
Capital allowances	
Trading income	

5b   In the year ended 31 December 2018 Knight Ltd expects taxable total profits of £420,000 and is expected to receive the exempt dividends from Sword Ltd of £10,000.

Requirement

Complete all the boxes below and state the first date by which any corporation tax should be paid in relation to the year ended 31 December 2018. Input the date in the format DD/MM/YYYY (eg, 03/04/2018 for 3 April 2018).

	£
Taxable total profits	
Exempt ABGH distributions	
Augmented profits	

Corporation tax due date	

LOs 5b, 5c, 5d

6a   Budding Ltd, an unquoted trading company, prepares accounts to 31 March and has no related 51% group companies. The draft accounting profits for the year ended 31 March 2018 are £165,000. The following items have been added or deducted in arriving at the draft accounting profit:

	Note	£
Depreciation		13,200
Bonuses	1	25,000
Qualifying donation	2	10,000
Exempt dividends received	3	6,750
Bank interest receivable		8,000

Notes:

(1)   Bonuses totalling £25,000 were paid in respect of this period on 2 February 2019. These were the first bonuses paid by the company.

(2)   The qualifying donation of £10,000 in the accounts comprises £8,300 paid during the accounting period and an accrual of £1,700 that the company had agreed to pay but was not paid until 10 June 2018.

(3)   Exempt dividends received from unrelated UK companies.

In addition, the following items have not yet been included in the accounts:

- Legal fees in relation to an issue of share capital (£1,750) and in relation to new employment contracts (£1,800).

- The company made no purchases or disposals of plant during the year ended 31 March 2018 but had a tax written down value on the main pool at 1 April 2017 of £800.

Requirement

Using the standard format below, compute Budding Ltd's taxable total profits for the year ended 31 March 2018. You should enter a number in each relevant box. If an amount is not taxable or no adjustment is required you must enter a zero or a dash into the relevant box.

	£
Trading income (W1)	
Non-trading loans	
Dividends	
Qualifying donation	
Taxable total profits	

W1 – Trading income

	£
Draft accounting profits	
Depreciation	
Bonuses	
Qualifying donation	
Exempt dividends received	
Bank interest receivable	
Legal fees	
Capital allowances	
Trading income	

6b   Assume that Budding Ltd has taxable total profits of £400,000 and has not received any dividends in the eight months ended 30 November 2018.

Requirement

You are required to state:

- the profits limit for the eight months ended 30 November 2018, that is used to determine whether Budding Ltd must pay corporation tax by instalments; and

- the first date by which any corporation tax should be paid in relation to the eight months ended 30 November 2018. Input the date in the format DD/MM/YYYY (eg, 03/04/2018 for 3 April 2018).

	£
The profits limit is	

Corporation tax due date	

LOs 5b, 5c, 5d

7a   Pedestal Ltd, an unquoted trading company, prepares accounts to 31 December and has no related 51% group companies. The draft accounting profits for the six months ended 31 December 2017 are £1,873,000. The following items have been added or deducted in arriving at the draft accounting profit:

	Note	£
Depreciation		80,900
HMRC interest payable	1	150
Donation	2	10,000
Client entertaining		6,300
Bank interest receivable		7,200

Notes:

(1)   HMRC interest was paid in respect of late corporation tax for the accounting period for the year ended 30 June 2017.

(2)   The donation of £10,000 paid during the accounting period related to a national registered charity (£8,000) and a political party (£2,000).

In addition, the following items have not yet been included in the accounts:

- The company issued £50,000 of debenture loan stock to fund the launch of a new product. The interest payable in respect of the loan stock was £2,500 for the six months ended 31 December 2017, and the company incurred legal fees in respect of the loan stock issue of £1,300.

- The company purchased machinery during the six months ended 31 December 2017 costing £50,000. The tax written down value on the main pool at 1 July 2017 was £120,000.

Requirement

Using the standard format below, compute Pedestal Ltd's taxable total profits for the six months ended 31 December 2017. You should enter a number in each relevant box. If an amount is not taxable or no adjustment is required you must enter a zero or a dash into the relevant box.

	£
Trading income (W1)	
Non-trading loans	
Qualifying donation	
Taxable total profits	

W1 – Trading income

	£
Draft accounting profits	
Depreciation	
HMRC interest payable	
Donation	
Client entertaining	
Bank interest receivable	
Loan stock	
Capital allowances	
Trading income	

7b   In the year ended 31 December 2018 Pedestal Ltd expects taxable total profits of £1,940,000 and is expected to receive £6,000 in dividends from unrelated UK companies and £1,000 from an unrelated USA company.

Requirement

Complete all the boxes below and state the first date by which any corporation tax should be paid in relation to the year ended 31 December 2018. Input the date in the format DD/MM/YYYY (eg, 03/04/2018 for 3 April 2018).

	£
Taxable total profits	
Exempt ABGH distributions	
Augmented profits	

Corporation tax due date	

LOs 5b, 5c, 5d

8a   Mayet Ltd, an unquoted trading company, prepares accounts to 30 June and has no related 51% group companies. The draft accounting profits for the year ended 30 June 2017 are £95,000. The following items have been added or deducted in arriving at the draft accounting profit:

	Note	£
Depreciation		4,500
Pension cost	1	10,000
Qualifying donation	2	14,000
Exempt dividends received	3	11,700
Bank interest receivable		13,000

Notes:

(1)   £8,000 of pension contribution was paid during the year ended 30 June 2017, with £2,000 accrued at the year end.

(2)   The qualifying donation of £14,000 in the accounts represents an amount paid to a charity in April 2017. A further £2,000 was paid to another charity in July 2016, but this amount had been accrued in the accounts of the previous accounting period.

(3)   Exempt dividends received from unrelated UK companies.

In addition, the following items have not yet been included in the accounts:

- The company wrote off a debt of £7,000 which related to an amount owing from a customer.

- The company purchased a new car with emissions of 55 g/km costing £12,300 during the year ended 30 June 2017. The tax written down value on the main pool at 1 July 2016 was £0.

Requirement

Using the standard format below, compute Mayet Ltd's taxable total profits for the year ended 30 June 2017. You should enter a number in each relevant box. If an amount is not taxable or no adjustment is required you must enter a zero or a dash into the relevant box.

	£
Trading income (W1)	
Non-trading loans	
Dividends	
Qualifying donation	
Taxable total profits	

W1 – Trading income

	£
Draft accounting profits	
Depreciation	
Pension cost	
Qualifying donation	
Exempt dividends received	
Bank interest receivable	
Debt write-offs	
Capital allowances	
Trading income	

8b In the year ended 30 June 2018 Mayet Ltd expects taxable total profits of £100,000 and is expected to receive exempt dividends of £10,000 from unrelated UK companies and exempt dividends of £2,000 from an unrelated Icelandic company.

Requirement

Complete all the boxes below and state the first date by which any corporation tax should be paid in relation to the year ended 30 June 2018. Input the date in the format DD/MM/YYYY (eg, 03/04/2018 for 3 April 2018).

	£
Taxable total profits	
Exempt ABGH distributions	
Augmented profits	

Corporation tax due date	

LOs 5b, 5c, 5d

9a Fonic Ltd, an unquoted trading company, prepares accounts to 30 September and has one wholly owned subsidiary. The draft accounting profits for the year ended 30 September 2017 are £852,000. The following items have been added or deducted in arriving at the draft accounting profit:

	Note	£
Depreciation		130,600
Profit on disposal	1	2,000
Property income	2	16,500
Exempt dividends received	3	10,800
Bank interest receivable		4,900
Entertaining	4	6,000

Notes:

(1) The profit was on disposal of a pool car (see below).

(2) Property income relates to rental of land next to the Fonic Ltd's factory. The rent received from 1 October 2016 to 31 August 2017 was £16,500, with a further £1,500 for the month of September 2017 outstanding as at 30 September 2017.

(3) Exempt dividends received from unrelated UK companies.

(4) Entertaining costs relate to a staff Christmas party costing £2,000 (£200 per employee) and client lunches totalling £4,000 (average cost per client £80).

In addition, the following item has not yet been included in the accounts:

• The company has not calculated any capital allowances for the accounting period. The only capital transaction was the disposal of the pool car. The proceeds on disposal of the car were £5,000 and the tax written down value on the main pool at 1 October 2016 was £1,500.

Requirement

Using the standard format below, compute Fonic Ltd's taxable total profits for the year ended 30 September 2017. You should enter a number in each relevant box. If an amount is not taxable or no adjustment is required you must enter a zero or a dash into the relevant box.

	£
Trading income (W1)	
Non-trading loans	
Dividends	
Property income	
Taxable total profits	

W1 – Trading income

	£
Draft accounting profits	
Depreciation	
Profit on disposal	
Property income	
Exempt dividends received	
Bank interest receivable	
Entertaining	
Capital allowances	
Trading income	

9b Assume that Fonic Ltd has taxable total profits of £600,000 and has not received any dividends in the year ended 30 September 2018.

Requirement

You are required to state:

- the profits limit for the year ended 30 September 2018, that is used to determine whether Fonic Ltd must pay corporation tax by instalments; and

- the first date by which any corporation tax should be paid in relation to the year ended 30 September 2018. Input the date in the format DD/MM/YYYY (eg, 03/04/2018 for 3 April 2018).

	£
The profits limit is	
Corporation tax due date	

LOs 5b, 5c, 5d

10a Selby Ltd, an unquoted trading company, prepares accounts to 31 December and has one wholly owned subsidiary. The draft accounting profits for the year ended 31 December 2017 are £534,000. The following items have been added or deducted in arriving at the draft accounting profit:

	Note	£
Depreciation		46,200
Loan interest payable	1	750
Qualifying donation	2	2,000
Pension contributions	3	56,000
Bank interest receivable		6,000

Notes.

(1) Interest payable on a loan to buy machinery.

(2) The qualifying donation of £2,000 in the accounts comprises £1,800 paid during the accounting period and an accrual of £200 that the company had agreed to pay but was not paid until 15 January 2018.

(3) The pension contributions of £56,000 comprise £34,000 paid by the company during the year and an additional £22,000 accrued at the year end.

In addition, the following items have not yet been included in the accounts:

- The company purchased machinery (costing £175,600) during the year ended 31 December 2017. The tax written down value on the main pool at 1 January 2017 was £75,000.

- Professional fees consisting of debt collection fees of £300 and a bank arrangement fee of £280 regarding the loan to buy the machinery.

Requirement

Using the standard format below, compute Selby Ltd's taxable total profits for the year ended 31 December 2017. You should enter a number in each relevant box. If an amount is not taxable or no adjustment is required you must enter a zero or a dash into the relevant box.

	£
Trading income (W1)	
Non-trading loans	
Qualifying donation	
Taxable total profits	

W1 – Trading income

	£
Draft accounting profits	
Depreciation	
Loan interest payable	
Qualifying donation	
Pension contributions	
Bank interest receivable	
Professional fees	
Capital allowances	
Trading income	

10b In the year ended 31 December 2018 Selby Ltd expects taxable total profits of £480,000 and is expected to receive no dividends.

Requirement

Complete all the boxes below and state the first date by which any corporation tax should be paid in relation to the year ended 31 December 2018. Input the date in the format DD/MM/YYYY (eg, 03/04/2018 for 3 April 2018).

	£
Taxable total profits	
Exempt ABGH distributions	
Augmented profits	

Corporation tax due date	

LOs 5b, 5c, 5d

Answer Bank

Answer Bank

Chapter 1: Ethics

1 B Professional intellect

   The five fundamental principles of the IESBA Code of Ethics are:

   - Integrity
   - Objectivity
   - Professional competence and due care
   - Confidentiality
   - Professional behaviour

2 B Integrity

   C Professional behaviour

3 A Objectivity

   D Confidentiality

   Sandra may be biased in her dealings with the company because of her relationship with Heather, and this threatens objectivity.

   Sandra may acquire information in her work which may be to Heather's advantage, but she must respect the confidentiality of such information.

4 A When he suspects a client of money laundering

   Richard must inform the NCA (National Crime Agency) if he suspects a client of money laundering.

   Confidentiality is required in respect of prospective or former clients, and must be maintained even in a social environment.

5 E Intimidation threat

   William is experiencing intimidation threats which occur when a professional accountant is deterred from acting objectively by threats, actual or perceived.

6 A Self-interest threat

   D Familiarity threat

   Roger is experiencing familiarity threats which occur when, because of a close relationship, a professional accountant becomes too sympathetic to the interests of others. As Jennifer's husband, he is himself also financially involved, which poses a self-interest threat.

   This question is from the sample paper issued by ICAEW.

7 A Freddy is laundering money through his business and as Florence is aware of this she is required to disclose it to the proper authorities.

   C Florence may be guilty of money-laundering offences as she has assisted Freddy in concealing the proceeds of crime.

   Florence should not discuss her decision to go to the authorities with Freddy. This would amount to tipping off which is in itself an offence under money laundering legislation.

   Florence may well have felt justified in increasing her fee for such risky work but in the circumstances this probably amounts to possessing the proceeds of a criminal activity which is another offence.

8 B Now

   D The firm's Money Laundering Reporting Officer

   Iqmal's responsibility is only to report to the MLRO. If he has reasonable suspicion, he should not try to obtain proof before reporting.

9   B   (1) to (3) only

         An innocent error in a tax return, unlike a deliberate error, would not give rise to proceeds of crime. Tax avoidance is not a crime and so cannot give rise to the proceeds of crime.

10   C   Timescale involved

         The other three are explicitly stated in the ICAEW Code as factors to consider.

11   A   Offence committed by Steven

        C   Offence committed by Trevor

         Steven has committed an offence under the legislation as he has acquired criminal property, the criminal property being the proceeds of tax evasion.

         Trevor has committed the offence of tipping off as he is aware that a suspicious activity report (SAR) may have been made by his firm's MLRO.

12   C   Advocacy threat

13   B   Self-review threat

14   B   The relationship that her firm has with the client

         The other three are explicitly stated in the ICAEW Code as factors to consider.

15   A   Tax evasion is illegal and tax avoidance is legal.

16   A   If the threat cannot be sufficiently reduced, the only acceptable course of action is to cease to act.

         This question is from the sample paper issued by ICAEW.

17   C   This is an example of legitimate tax planning so is tax avoidance. The others are all examples of tax evasion.

         This question is from the sample paper issued by ICAEW.

1   B   HMRC statements of practice

           A Finance Act is an Act of Parliament and is therefore a source of law. Case law generally sets a precedent which must be followed unless overruled on appeal or superseded by legislation. Statutory instruments are a form of delegated legislation which are a form of law. Statements of practice are merely a statement of HMRC's interpretation of the law.

2   A   Progressive taxation

       C   Direct taxation

           A system whereby the overall proportion of taxation increases as income rises is known as a progressive system. Originally income tax represented 15% of Pauline's income. After her pay rise it had risen to 20%.

           National insurance contributions are a form of direct taxation.

       This question is from the sample paper issued by ICAEW.

3   B   Efficiency principle

       D   Indirect taxation

           The efficiency principle is concerned with the cost (to a government) of collection of tax being low in relation to the tax raised. The ability to pay principle is concerned with the ability of the taxpayer to pay the tax.

           VAT is a form of indirect taxation.

4   C   Unit principle

           This is an example of a unit tax as opposed to VAT which is a value based tax. A unit tax is levied at a flat rate per item regardless of value. It cannot be considered a neutral tax as only supermarkets have to charge it.

5   B   Statutory instruments

           While the Budget forms the basis for the Finance Act each year, it is not in itself a form of legislation. Statutory instruments are the biggest single source of tax law each year. Extra-statutory concessions, as their name implies, are not statutory documents. Neither are statements of practice.

6   C   (1), (3), (4) and (5) only

           As an employee Diana will be liable to income tax and national insurance contributions. As an individual Diana could pay capital gains tax on the disposal of an asset. As an individual Diana must incur VAT in her day to day life as the final consumer. As an individual Diana cannot personally pay corporation tax.

7   C   (2), (3) and (5) only

           Each partner is liable to tax on his share of income and gains of the partnership, but not for tax on the shares of income and gains of the other partners.

8   C   (1), (2) and (4) only

           (1)   Collect and administer direct taxes
           (2)   Collect and administer indirect taxes
           (4)   Collect repayments of student loans

       This question is from the sample paper issued by ICAEW.

9   C   Case law can be superseded by further statutory legislation.

Many judgements from tax cases are precedent for future cases which means they must be followed unless superseded by legislation or the decision of a higher court. Therefore, this is not guidance. There is also no 12-month time limit and subsequent legislation can change the law.

10   D   Tax legislation, commonly in the form of Regulations, containing detailed provisions

HMRC manuals are published by HMRC primarily for the guidance of its own staff.
Statements of practice set out HMRC's interpretation of tax legislation.
Extra-statutory concessions provide a relaxation of the strict legal position of tax legislation.

1   What is his personal allowance for 2017/18? £ [2,625]

	£
Personal allowance	11,500
Less (£117,750 – £100,000) = £17,750 × 1/2	(8,875)
Reduced personal allowance	2,625

2   What is Mackenzie's total income for tax liability for 2017/18? £ [5,133]

	£
Tax on non-savings income £25,565 × 20%	5,113
Tax on savings income – savings income nil rate band £1,000 × 0%	0
Tax on savings income £100 × 20%	20
Income tax liability	5,133

3   The married couple's allowance due to the couple for 2017/18 will initially be given to

B   Grainne (as Grainne has the higher net income)

The allowance due to the couple to give relief at 10% is

F   £8,445 (available based on the age of the elder spouse)

4   A   £917

Extend BRB by Gift Aid = £33,500 + (£720 × 100/80) = £34,400

Tax on non-savings income			£
£34,400	×	20%	6,880
£1,130	×	40%	452

Tax on dividend income			
£5,000	×	0%	0
£1,200	×	32.5%	390
£41,730			7,722

Less tax already paid	
PAYE	(6,805)
Tax payable	917

5   C   £20,013

Tax on dividend income			£
£5,000	×	0%	0
£28,500	×	7.5%	2,138
£55,000	×	32.5%	17,875
£88,500			20,013

6   B   £774

£8,445 (MCA available as one spouse is at least 83 by 5 April 2018) × 11/12 (restricted for complete tax months prior to marriage) × 10%

7   What is Glenn's total income tax liability for 2017/18? £ [5,798]

	£
Tax on non-savings income £28,500 × 20%	5,700
Tax on dividend income – dividend nil rate band £5,000 × 0%	0
Tax on dividend income £300 × 32.5%	98
Income tax liability	5,798

£300 of dividend income is taxed at 32.5% as the cumulative income taxed so far is £33,500 (£28,490 + £5,000) which utilises the basic rate band of £33,500.

8 What is Mabel's income tax liability for 2017/18? £ | 7,536 |

Taxable income (all savings)		£39,000
Tax		£
£5,000	× 0%	0
£500	× 0%	0
£28,000	× 20%	5,600
£1,320	(£1,056 × $^{100}/_{80}$) × 20% (extended band)	264
£4,180	× 40%	1,672
£39,000		
Income tax liability		7,536

9 B He receives basic rate tax relief at source by paying net of basic rate income tax

  F He receives higher rate tax relief by extending the basic rate band

10 B £10,135

	£
Personal allowance	11,500
Less abatement	
1/2 × (£102,730 – £100,000)	(1,365)
Reduced personal allowance	10,135

11 C £600

	£		£
Tax on non-savings income	3,000	× 20%	600
Tax on saving income:			
– in savings starting rate band	2,000	× 0%	0
	5,000		
–savings income nil rate band	800	× 0%	0
	5,800		
Tax on dividend income:			
– dividend nil rate band	1,500	× 0%	0
	7,300		
Income tax liability			600

12 C £4,000

  Dividend income is the top slice of income hence £33,500 – £30,000 = £3,500 falls in the dividend ordinary rate band, but this and a further £1,500 is covered by the dividend nil rate band. Therefore, £4,000 (£9,000 – £5,000) is taxed at 32.5%.

13 C In 2017/18 the Gift Aid payment will have no impact on Maalik's income tax liability.

  Maalik is a basic rate taxpayer in 2017/18 so increasing the upper limit of his basic rate band will have no impact on the calculation of his income tax liability.

14 What is Bussola's income tax liability for 2017/18? £ | 7,566 |

	£		£
Tax on non-savings income	210	× 20%	42
Tax on saving income:			
– in savings starting rate band	4,790	× 0%	0
	5,000		
– savings income nil rate band	500	× 0%	0
– in savings basic rate band	28,000	× 20%	5,600
	33,500		
– in savings higher rate band	4,810	× 40%	1,924
	38,310		
Income tax liability			7,566

15   What is Manav's income tax liability for 2017/18? £ 3,563

Tax	£
£17,015 × 20%	3,403
£1,000 × 0%	0
£800 × 20%	160
Income tax liability	3,563

16   What is Frederick's income tax payable under self-assessment for 2017/18? £ 63

Taxable income	£15,815

	£
20% on £15,815	3,163
Less PAYE	(3,100)
Income tax payable	63

This question is from the sample paper issued by ICAEW.

17   A   £0 – Allocated to Bertha as she has the higher net income.

This question is from the sample paper issued by ICAEW.

18   What is Darcy's personal allowance for 2017/18? £ 0

The personal allowance will be zero for any additional rate taxpayer.

19   D   £61,880

	£
Non-savings income	133,000
Savings income	27,600
Dividends	15,000
Taxable income	175,600

	£
£33,500 × 20%	6,700
£99,500 × 40%	39,800
£133,000	
£17,000 × 40%	6,800
£150,000	
£10,600 × 45%	4,770
£5,000 × 0%	0
£10,000 × 38.1%	3,810
£175,600	
Income tax liability	61,880

Dave has no savings income nil rate band as he is an additional rate taxpayer. He does benefit from the dividend nil rate band.

20   What is Diane's personal allowance for 2017/18? £ 2,500

	£
Personal allowance	11,500
Less (£118,000 – £100,000) × 1/2	(9,000)
Restricted personal allowance	2,500

The personal allowance is abated due to the level of net income.

21   What is Sandra's personal allowance for 2017/18? £ 0

With net income exceeding £123,000, the PA is reduced to zero.

22 What is Geoff's income tax liability for 2017/18? £ [2,660]

	£
Non-savings income £14,450 × 20%	2,890
less tax reducer for marriage allowance £1,150 × 20%	(230)
Geoff's income tax liability	2,660

The election is possible because Geoff is a basic rate taxpayer and Jessica pays no income tax.

23 D   No election can be made to transfer any part of Richard's personal allowance to Leanne as she is a higher rate taxpayer.

24 What is Sarah's married couple's allowance for 2017/18 on which 10% tax relief is given?
£ [7,945]

	£
Married couple's allowance	8,445
Less (£29,000 – £28,000) × ½	(500)
Reduced married couple's allowance	7,945

The MCA is given because of Arthur's age. However, Sarah is the taxpayer entitled to claim the MCA since she has the higher net income in 2017/18 and the couple were married on or after 5 December 2005. The MCA is restricted because of the level of Sarah's income.

25 What is Shelia's married couple's allowance for 2017/18 on which 10% tax relief is given?
£ [3,260]

	£
Married couple's allowance	8,445
Less (£39,300 – £28,000) × ½ = £5,650 but restricted	(5,185)
Reduced married couple's allowance	3,260

The MCA is given because of Archie's age. However, Shelia is the taxpayer entitled to claim the MCA since she has the higher net income in 2017/18 and the couple were married on or after 5 December 2005.

The MCA is restricted because of the level of Shelia's income, but cannot be less than £3,260.

Chapter 4: Employment income

1   A   606L

	£
Personal allowance	11,500
Less taxable benefits	(4,208)
Less underpaid tax £246 × 100/20	(1,230)
	6,062
PAYE code	606L

2   A   730L

	£
Personal allowance	11,500
Less underpaid tax £840 × 100/20	(4,200)
	7,300
PAYE code	730L

3   PAYE code   K604

	£
Personal allowance	11,500
Less taxable benefits	(17,550)
Net allowances	(6,050)

Remove the last digit (gives 605) and deduct 1.

PAYE code	K604

4   A   K126

	£
Personal allowance	11,500
Less taxable benefit	(12,775)
Net allowances	(1,275)

Remove the last digit (gives 127) and deduct 1.

Hence the code is K126.

5   What is Jacob's PAYE code for 2017/18?   694   L

	£
Personal allowance	11,500
Less taxable benefit	(4,560)
Net allowances	6,940

Remove the last digit and add L

6   B   842L

	£
Personal allowance	11,500
Less deduction (£1,232 × 100/40)	(3,080)
Net allowances	8,420

Remove the last digit and add L.

This question is from the sample paper issued by ICAEW.

Principles of Taxation: Question Bank

Chapter 5: Trading profits

1   A   Amy has just sold a house that she bought three months ago. She has spent £40,000 to make the property more attractive to potential purchasers. Amy has not lived in this house.

    D   Dante has an interest in vintage cars. He has just sold a car that he has been renovating for the last six months. This is the seventh renovated car that he has sold in the last two years.

This question is from the sample paper issued by ICAEW.

2   B   Provision of own equipment
    E   Correction of own work

3   A   The number of transactions

    C   Changes to the asset

Interval of time between purchase and sale – a **short** length of ownership would indicate trade.

Correction of own work – this is not one of the badges of trade.

4   D   To be sold at a profit

The nature of the asset would suggest a trading motive.

Chapter 6: Capital allowances

1   B   The maximum capital allowances that Nina will receive in respect of the purchase of the photocopier in the year ended 31 December 2017 are £2,070.

£2,300 × 90% = £2,070

F   The maximum capital allowances that Nina will receive in respect of the purchase of the car in the year ended 31 December 2017 are £373.

18% × £2,300 × 90% = £373

2   A   The maximum capital allowances that Aasia will receive in respect of the purchase of the photocopier in the period ended 31 December 2017 are £3,000 as it is covered by the AIA (pro rated to £200,000 × 10/12 = £166,667).

F   The maximum capital allowances that Aasia will receive in respect of the purchase of the car in the period ended 31 December 2017 are £450.

18% × 10/12 × £3,000 = £450

3   A   The maximum capital allowances available on the computer in the period to 31 December 2017 are £5,000 as it is covered by the AIA (pro rated to £200,000 × 4/12 = £66,667).

F   The maximum capital allowances available on the car in the period to 31 December 2017 are £792.

£13,200 × 18% × 4/12 = £792

4   C   The maximum capital allowance claim available to Barbara for the period is £10,560.

£13,200 (covered by AIA) × 80% = £10,560

5   Expenditure on new cars emitting CO_2 of not more than 75g/km qualifies for the annual investment allowance (AIA) of 100%.

B   Incorrect

The expenditure qualifies for a first year allowance (FYA) of 100%.

Capital expenditure is not allowable in computing trading profits but will always result in capital allowances.

D   Incorrect

It will **often** result in capital allowances but not always (eg, cost of a new office building)

6   What are Murphy's maximum capital allowances for the period ended 31 December 2017?
£ 219,020

Y/e 31.12.17	FYA £	Main pool £	Allowances £
Acquisitions (FYA):			
1.9.17 Low emission car	16,500		
FYA @ 100%	(16,500)		16,500
	0		
Acquisitions (AIA):			
1.7.17 Machinery		214,000	
AIA		(200,000)	200,000
		14,000	
WDA @ 18%		(2,520)	2,520
TWDV c/f		11,480	
Allowances			219,020

7   What are the partnership's maximum capital allowances for the year ended 31 March 2018?

    £ [3,236]

		£
Murray's car	£17,000 × 18% × 60%	1,836
Nuri's car – balancing allowance (£8,000 – £6,000)		
Balancing allowance	£2,000 × 70%	1,400
		3,236

8   C   £3,600

    The balancing allowance for full business use is £4,800 (£15,000 – £10,200)

    This is restricted to the business proportion £3,600 (75% × £4,800)

9   Capital allowances £ [20,000]

Y/e 31.12.17	FYA £	Main pool £	Allowances £
Acquisitions (FYA):			
20.3.17 Low emission car	8,000		
FYA @ 100%	(8,000)		8,000
	0		
Acquisitions (AIA):			
12.2.17 Computer		10,000	
1.5.17 Office furniture		2,000	
AIA		(12,000)	12,000
TWDV c/f		0	
Allowances			20,000

10 Capital allowances   £ [1,458]

1.9.17 – 31.5.18	Car ≤130g/km £		Allowances £
Addition	18,000		
WDA 18% × 9/12	(2,430)	× 60%	1,458
	15,570		

    This question is from the sample paper issued by ICAEW.

11 C   Balancing allowance of £1,750

y/e 31.3.18	Private use car £		Allowances £
TWDV brought forward	17,000		
Disposal	(14,500)		
Balancing allowance	2,500	× 70%	1,750

12 What is the maximum amount of capital allowances that can be claimed in the year ended 31 May 2018 relating to this car? £ [3,240]

    The car has a writing down allowance of 18% per annum as it will go in the main pool. This is not restricted for private use by an **employee**.

13 B   £1,440

1.10.17 – 31.3.18 (six months)	Main pool £	Allowances £
Addition	16,000	
WDA @ 18% × 6/12	(1,440)	1,440
TWDV c/f	14,560	

14 A £8,560

	Main pool £	Allowances £
1.4.17 – 31.12.17 (nine months)		
TWDV b/f	560	
Acquisitions (AIA):		
Computer	8,000	
AIA (£200,000 × 9/12 = £150,000)	(8,000)	8,000
	560	
Write-off of small pool (£1,000 × 9/12 = £750)	(560)	560
TWDV c/f	0	
Allowances		8,560

As the small pool is less than the pro rated minimum balance of £750, it may be written off in full.

15 What are the maximum capital allowances that can be claimed by Matthew for the year ended 31 December 2017? £ [342   ]

As the business continues there is no balancing adjustment in the main pool on the disposal of the machine. (Once the pool drops to £1,000 or less in a later year, the whole pool may be written off.)

	Main pool £	Allowances £
Y/e 31.12.17		
TWDV brought forward	2,300	
Disposal	(400)	
	1,900	
WDA @ 18%	(342)	342
TWDV carried forward	1,558	

16 What are the maximum capital allowances that can be claimed by Max for the year ended 30 September 2017? £ [3,870   ]

	Main pool £	Allowances £
Y/e 30.9.17		
TWDV brought forward	25,400	
Disposal (use cost as sale proceeds exceed cost)	(3,900)	
	21,500	
WDA @ 18%	(3,870)	3,870
TWDV carried forward	17,630	

17 C £11,160

	FYA £	Main pool £	Allowances £
1.10.17 – 31.3.18 (6 months)			
TWDV brought forward		24,000	
WDA @ 18% × 6/12		(2,160)	2,160
Additions (FYA)	9,000		
FYA @ 100% (low emission car)	(9,000)		9,000
TWDV carried forward	0	21,840	
Total allowances			11,160

The FYA is not pro rated for short accounting periods.

Note: Unless you are told otherwise, assume no private use of assets by the owner(s) of a business.

18   B   £87,208

	Main pool £	Allowances £
1.8.17 – 31.12.17 (5 months)		
Acquisitions (AIA):		
23.11.17 Machine	135,000	
AIA (£200,000 × 5/12)	(83,333)	83,333
	51,667	
WDA @ 18% × 5/12	(3,875)	3,875
TWDV c/f	47,792	
Allowances		87,208

19   B   Car with emission of 125g/km costing £14,000 on 10 June 2017 with 20% private use by one of the employees

20   What are the maximum capital allowances that can be claimed by Jamie for the year ended 31 January 2018? £ [4,626]

	Main pool £	Allowances £
Y/e 31.1.18		
TWDV brought forward	31,000	
Disposal	(5,300)	
	25,700	
WDA @ 18%	(4,626)	4,626
TWDV c/f	21,074	

21   What are the maximum capital allowances that can be claimed by Janice on the machine for the year ended 31 December 2017? £ [203,600]

	Main pool £	Allowances £
Y/e 31.12.17		
Acquisitions (AIA):		
1.5.17 Machine	220,000	
AIA	(200,000)	200,000
	20,000	
WDA @ 18%	(3,600)	3,600
TWDV c/f	16,400	
Allowances		203,600

Chapter 7: Trading profits – basis of assessment

1   What are the trading profits assessable on Rafael in 2017/18?

£ | 39,300

y/e 30 June 2017	Total £	Rafael £	Saeed £	Tadeo £
Salary	10,000		10,000	
Interest	6,100	3,000	1,200	1,900
Balance 1:1:1	108,900	36,300	36,300	36,300
	125,000	39,300	47,500	38,200

Rafael has taxable trading profits of £39,300 for the year ended 30 June 2017. As the partnership is not new this will be taxed on Rafael in 2017/18.

2   A   £38,000

   CYB

   Basis period y/e 30 April 2016 = £38,000

   E   £50,000

   Final tax year (2017/18)

	£
Basis period 1 May 2016 to 30 November 2017	
y/e 30 April 2017	34,000
p/e 30 November 2017	23,000
	57,000
Less overlap profits	(7,000)
	50,000

3   B   Jabir £32,958   Kadin £28,292

y/e 31 August 2018	Total £	Jabir £	Kadin £
Salary	8,000	8,000	
PSR 1:1	97,000	48,500	48,500
	105,000	56,500	48,500
2017/18 opening years (7/12)		32,958	28,292

   First tax year (2017/18)

   Actual basis

   Basis period 1 September 2017 to 5 April 2018

4   B   First accounts are 6 months ended 5 April 2018 with future accounts to 5 April

   First year 2017/18 = p/e 5 April 2018

   Second year 2018/19 = y/e 5 April 2019 etc

5   What are the trading profits assessable on Cliff in 2017/18? £ | 49,500

y/e 30 September 2017	Total £	Val £	Cliff £	Frank £
Interest on capital (5%)	6,000	2,500	1,500	2,000
PSR 1:1:1	144,000	48,000	48,000	48,000
	150,000	50,500	49,500	50,000

   CYB applies as the partnership has traded for many years.

6   B   Tom £83,333   Dick £36,667

Y/e 31 Oct 2017	Total £	Tom £	Dick £
Salary	10,000	10,000	
PSR 2:1	110,000	73,333	36,667
	120,000	83,333	36,667

CYB applies as the partnership has traded for many years.

7   What is Raanan's trading profit assessment for 2017/18? £ [7,000]

Final tax year (2017/18)

	£
Basis period 1 February 2017 to 31 December 2018	
P/e 31 December 2017	15,000
Less unrelieved overlap profits	(8,000)
	7,000

Penultimate tax year (2016/17)
CYB
Basis period y/e 31 January 2017

8   C   £1,300

First tax year (2015/16)
Actual basis
Basis period 1 January 2016 to 5 April 2016

$3/12 \times £6,000 = £1,500$

Second tax year (2016/17)
12 month period ending in the tax year
Basis period 1 January 2016 to 31 December 2016

Year ended 31 December 2016 = £6,000

Overlap profits

1 January 2016 to 5 April 2016 = £1,500

Final tax year (2017/18)

	£
Basis period 1 January 2017 to 28 February 2018	
P/e 28 February 2018	2,800
Less unrelieved overlap profits	(1,500)
	1,300

9   D   £21,000

Final tax year (2017/18)

	£
Basis period 1 October 2016 to 30 April 2017	
P/e 30 April 2017	25,000
Less unrelieved overlap profits	(4,000)
	21,000

Penultimate tax year (2016/17)
Basis period y/e 30 September 2016

10   B   £18,000

First tax year (2017/18)
Actual basis
Basis period 1 July 2017 to 5 April 2018 = $9/12 \times £24,000 = £18,000$

11 B   £18,000

> **First tax year (2017/18)**
> Actual basis
> Basis period 1 July 2017 to 5 April 2018
>
> **Second tax year (2018/19)**
> CYB
> Basis period y/e 30 June 2018
>
> Overlap profits 1 July 2017 to 5 April 2018 = 9/12 × £24,000 = £18,000

12 B   Taxable trading profits for 2016/17 are £5,000

D   Taxable trading profits for 2017/18 are £22,500

> **First tax year (2016/17)**
> Actual basis
> Basis period 1 January 2017 to 5 April 2017
> 3/6 × £10,000   £5,000
>
> **Second tax year (2017/18)**
> Period of accounts in second tax year is less than 12 months
> Basis period 1 January 2017 to 31 December 2017

		£
P/e 30 June 2017		10,000
1 July 2017 to 31 Dec 2017	6/12 × £25,000	12,500
		22,500

13 A   £28,000 is taxable in 2017/18, representing the period 6 April 2017 to 5 April 2018.

> 12/18 × £42,000 – no accounting period ending in second tax year so actual basis applies.

14 What is the taxable trading income for 2017/18? £ | 85,000 |

> **First tax year (2017/18)**
>
> Actual basis: 1 July 2017 to 5 April 2018 = £60,000 + (3/12 × £100,000)

15 What are Ray's overlap profits? £ | 25,000 |

> First year actual basis: 1 July 2017 to 5 April 2018 = £60,000 + (3/12 × £100,000)
>
> Second year CYB year ended 31 December 2018 = £100,000
>
> Overlap = 1 January 2018 to 5 April 2018 = 3/12 × £100,000 = £25,000

16 D   Amber £145,000   Betty £95,000

	Total £	Amber £	Betty £
6 months to 30 June			
PSR (£120,000) 2:1	120,000	80,000	40,000
6 months to 31 December			
Salary (× 6/12)	10,000	10,000	
PSR (£110,000) 1:1	110,000	55,000	55,000
	240,000	145,000	95,000

17 What are the trading profits assessable on Aubrey in 2017/18? £ | 50,750 |

	Total £	Aubrey £	Elaine £
Y/e 30 September 2017			
Interest on capital (5%)	3,500	2,500	1,000
PSR 1:1	96,500	48,250	48,250
	100,000	50,750	49,250

CYB applies as the partnership has traded for many years.

18 D £30,000

	Total £	David £	Doreen £
Y/e 30 June 2018 PSR 2:1	120,000	80,000	40,000

First year actual basis (2017/18)

1 July 2017 to 5 April 2018

9/12 × £40,000 = £30,000

19 What is Florian's taxable trading income for 2017/18? £ 14,820

2016/17 = year ended 31 January 2017 = £21,200

2017/18 = remaining profits less overlap = £17,430 – 2,610 = £14,820

20 B £39,990

	Total £	Leroy £	Annabelle £
Interest on capital (5%)	2,900	1,750	1,150
Balance (2:3)	95,600	38,240	57,360
Tax adjusted profit	98,500	39,990	58,510

This question is from the sample paper issued by ICAEW.

21 B £45,607

2016/17 (1.1.17 to 5.4.17)

2017/18 (1.3.17 to 28.2.18)

Profits 2017/18

12/14 × £53,208 = £45,607

This question is from the sample paper issued by ICAEW.

22 D £33,100

	£	£
Total receipts	63,000	
Less receipt from sale of car as not taxable as trading income	(3,000)	
		60,000
Total payments	27,000	
Less interest paid on bank loan (max £500)	(100)	
		(26,900)
Taxable trading profit		33,100

23 A £24,300

Taxable trading profits for the 10 months ended 30 April 2018 are £27,000 (£58,000 – £31,000).

The opening year rules apply. In 2017/18 tax the actual profits from 1 July 2017 to 5 April 2018.

Profits 2017/18

9/10 × £27,000 = £24,300

1   A   Class 1 primary

     C   Class 2

        Sho's trading profits are below the lower profits limit for Class 4 NIC.

2   B   Wagner Ltd will pay Class 4 NICs on the profits of £80,000 – Incorrect

        Companies do not pay Class 4 NIC.

     C   George will pay Class 1 primary NICs on his earnings of £15,000 – Correct

        He is below state pension age and his earnings are above the primary threshold.

     F   Wagner Ltd will pay Class 1 secondary NICs on total employee remuneration of £65,000 – Incorrect

        Dividends are not earnings. The company will therefore be liable to secondary Class 1 NICs on £20,000 + £15,000 = £35,000.

3   Steven's Class 4 NICs (on trade profits only) for 2017/18 are £ [390]

     (£12,500 – £8,164) × 9% = £390

4   B   £3,355

	£
9% (£45,000 – £8,164)	3,315
2% (£47,000 – £45,000)	40
	3,355

5   B   £1,213

		£
Class 2	52 × £2.85	148
Class 4	9% (£20,000 – £8,164)	1,065
		1,213

     This question is from the sample paper issued by ICAEW.

6   What are the Class 1 secondary contributions payable by Ball Ltd in 2017/18 in respect of Lena?
£ [4,305]

	£
Class 1 secondary (£38,862 + 500 – £8,164) × 13.8%	4,305

Class 1 secondary contributions are not paid on the car benefit but are paid on the vouchers. The car benefit gives rise to a liability to Class 1A NIC.

7   What are the Class 1A contributions payable by Ball Ltd in 2017/18 in respect of Lena?
£ [690]

	£
Class 1A £5,000 × 13.8%	690

Class 1A contributions are not paid on the vouchers (Class 1 secondary contributions are payable).

8   B   Boris will have Class 1 primary contributions deducted from his wages – Incorrect

     C   Jinx Ltd must pay Class 1 secondary contributions in relation to Boris's earnings – Correct

        When an individual reaches state pension age he stops paying Class 1 primary contributions but his employer must still pay Class 1 secondary contributions.

9   What is the total national insurance liability of the company for 2017/18? £ | 3,788 |

Only liability is to Class 1 secondary NIC. Cobalt Ltd is not entitled to the employment allowance as the company has only one director and no other employees.

(£35,610 – £8,164) × 13.8% = £3,788

10   C   £5,497

		£
Class 1 secondary	(£45,000 – £8,164) × 13.8%	5,083
Class 1 A	£3,000 × 13.8%	414
		5,497

11   What is the total national insurance liability of Belinda for 2017/18? £ | 3,893 |

	£
Class 1 primary	
(£3,300 – £680) × 12% = £314 × 11 months	3,454
(£3,750 – £680) × 12% = £368 × 1 month	368
(£7,300 – £3,750) × 2% = £71 × 1 month	71
Total	3,893

This question is from the sample paper issued by ICAEW.

12   What are the Class 1 secondary contributions payable by Pirate Ltd in 2017/18 in respect of Sue?
£ | 276 |

	£
Class 1 secondary (aged under 21) (£47,000 – £45,000) × 13.8%	276

Class 1 secondary contributions are not paid on benefits. Taxable benefits (the car) give rise to a liability to Class 1A NIC.

13   What are the Class 1A contributions payable by Pirate Ltd in 2017/18 in respect of Sue?
£ | 414 |

	£
Class 1A £3,000 × 13.8%	414

14   What are the Class 1 secondary contributions payable by Hans in 2017/18 in respect of Olga?
£ | 841 |

	£
Class 1 secondary (£36,000 – £8,164) × 13.8% - £3,000	841

The employment allowance is available even though there is only one employee, as the employer, Hans is a sole trader and not a company.

15   What are the Class 1 secondary contributions payable by Rene Ltd in 2017/18 in respect of Kamal?
£ | 0 |

Kamal is an apprentice under 25 years old and his salary does not exceed the apprentice upper secondary threshold of £45,000.

16   What are the Class 1 primary contributions payable by Kamal in 2017/18? £ | 1,420 |

	£
Class 1 primary (£20,000 – £8,164) × 12%	1,420

1   D   Partners individually

The partnership is not taxable in its own right; rather it is an amalgamation of individuals effectively taxed as sole traders. Neither are partners taxed jointly. Every individual is liable to capital gains tax independently. As the asset is owned by all the partners, each partner must declare his or her share of any gain on their own self-assessment return.

2   A   15 March 2018

The date of disposal for capital gains purposes is the date on which the contract for disposal becomes unconditional. In this case the contract became unconditional on the date contracts were exchanged. The date legal title passes, physical possession is obtained, or payment is made are all irrelevant.

3   C   Stamp duty land tax paid on the purchase of land may be deducted as part of cost on a subsequent disposal of the land.

Assets which are inherited are treated as being acquired by the donee at their probate value ie, at their value at the time of the donor's death. This is sometimes known as the tax-free uplift on death.

Wasting chattels are always exempt from CGT. The £6,000 rule applies to non-wasting chattels.

Where an asset is not sold at arm's length the proceeds are deemed to be market value at the time of sale or gift.

4   A   £(7,800)

As a non-wasting asset, the chattel rules apply. As it was sold at a loss, actual proceeds are substituted by deemed proceeds of £6,000 to restrict the loss.

	£
Deemed proceeds	6,000
Less auctioneer's fees	(800)
Net sale proceeds	5,200
Less cost	(13,000)
Loss	(7,800)

5   B   Gain of £4,500 on the disposal of a caravan – Exempt

D   Gain of £1,000 on the sale of a sculpture. The sculpture originally cost £4,000 – Exempt

The caravan is a wasting chattel which is an exempt asset.

The sculpture is a non-wasting chattel, which is a chargeable asset. However, as it was both bought and sold for less than £6,000, it is specifically exempt.

6   D   £8,090

The chair is a non-wasting asset and is liable to capital gains tax subject to the chattel rules. As it was purchased for less than £6,000 and sold for more than £6,000 there is a marginal gain. The gain is the lower of the actual gain and 5/3 × (Gross proceeds – £6,000):

Actual gain = £11,150 – £560 – £2,500 = £8,090

5/3 × (£11,150 – £6,000) = £8,583

7 C His unused annual exempt amount from 2016/17 – No effect

E Becoming a higher-rate tax payer for the first time – Increases capital gains tax payable

An unused annual exempt amount is wasted and cannot be carried forward to the next tax year. Therefore this will have no effect on David's capital gains tax liability.

The rate of his capital gains tax is 20% once he is a higher rate taxpayer. As a basic rate taxpayer to the extent that there is an amount of the basic rate band remaining after deducting taxable income, that amount of gains will be taxed at only 10%.

8 A Partners individually

The partnership is not taxable in its own right; rather it is an amalgamation of individuals effectively taxed as sole traders. Neither are partners taxed jointly. Every individual is liable to capital gains tax independently. As the asset is owned by all the partners, each partner must declare his share of any gain on his own self-assessment return.

9 Chargeable gain £ | 457,840 |

	£	£
Gross sale proceeds		642,000
Less: original cost (Dec 1997)	176,000	
stamp duty land tax (1% × 176,000)	1,760	
new bathroom	6,400	
		(184,160)
Chargeable gain		457,840

10 A £10,808

The painting is a non-wasting chattel and is liable to capital gains tax subject to the chattel rules. As it was purchased for less than £6,000 and sold for more than £6,000, there is a marginal gain. The gain is the lower of the actual gain and 5/3 × (Gross proceeds – £6,000):

Actual gain = £14,150 – £142 – £3,200 = £10,808

5/3 × (£14,150 – £6,000) = £13,583

11 C A rare collection of snakes worth £320,000

D £10,000 of National Savings Certificates

Shares held in an unquoted trading company are not exempt from capital gains. A diamond necklace is a non-wasting asset and is therefore subject to the chattel rules. It is only fully exempt if it is both bought and sold for less than £6,000. That clearly would not apply in this case. Snakes are a wasting chattel and are therefore exempt. National Savings Certificates are specifically exempted.

12 C Gift to a friend of a painting worth £1,000,000

Gifts on death are not chargeable disposals.

National Savings Certificates are an exempt asset. As it is not a chargeable asset, there cannot be a chargeable disposal.

A gift of any capital asset to a charity is not a chargeable disposal.

13 B 1 September 2017

The date of disposal for capital gains purposes is the date on which the contract for disposal becomes unconditional. In this case the contract became unconditional on the date the valuation took place. The date contracts are exchanged, legal title passes, physical possession is obtained, or payment is made are all irrelevant.

14   C   Assets which are inherited are treated as being acquired by the donee at their value at the time of the donor's death.

CGT is chargeable on individuals and partners in a partnership. Companies pay corporation tax on their gains.

Stamp duty land tax is an allowable cost on the subsequent disposal of an asset.

Indexation allowance is not available to individuals.

15   B   Gain of £2,500 on the disposal of a car – Exempt

      D   Gain of £3,000 on the sale of a greyhound – Exempt

A car is an exempt asset.

The greyhound is a wasting chattel and is therefore exempt.

16   A   NSPCC, a registered charity. Charities are specifically exempt from CGT.

17   D   The gift of an antique table valued at £40,000 to Gordon's daughter on his death

18   C   £105,300

Not the repairs as they are not an enhancement expenditure.

£(100,000 + 2,500 + 2,800) = £105,300

This question is from the sample paper issued by ICAEW.

19   B   A racehorse purchased as an investment by Max

      D   A caravan, purchased by David for use on family holidays

An asset used only for business purposes and eligible for capital allowances is specifically treated as a non-wasting chattel.

Goodwill is not a chattel as it is not **tangible** moveable property.

20   Javier sold a painting at auction and received £5,900 after deducting auctioneer's fees of £310. The painting had originally cost him £3,500.

      A   Chargeable – This is a disposal of a non wasting chattel with GROSS sale proceeds of more than £6,000, so chargeable.

Savion received £2,600 for some shares that he sold after deducting £150 of fees. The shares originally cost him £800.

      C   Chargeable – Shares are not chattels and so not subject to the £6,000 rules.

21   B   £500

The brooch is a non-wasting asset and is liable to capital gains tax subject to the chattel rules.

Gain is £(6,200 – 4,000) = £2,200 but restricted to

(Gross sale proceeds – £6,000) × 5/3 = (£6,300 – £6,000) × 5/3 = £500

22   D   £(900)

	£
Deemed gross sale proceeds	6,000
Less selling expenses	(200)
Less cost	(6,700)
Allowable loss	(900)

23   C   A gift of antique jewellery worth £25,000 by Robert, to his daughter as a wedding gift

Disposal to an art gallery is an exempt disposal.

A registered charity is an exempt person.

Gilt-edged securities are an exempt asset.

24   C   Townsend lost an antique ring valued at £8,000 and received a cheque from the insurance company for that sum

       D   Toshi sold a painting for £5,000. It was given to him several years when his grandfather died. At that time it was worth £6,400

25   Fraser's chargeable gain on disposal of the brooch is £ | 1,400 |

	£
Gross sale proceeds	8,200
Less auctioneer's fees	(300)
Net sale proceeds	7,900
Less: original cost (July 2000)	(6,100)
enhancement expenditure (September 2004)	(400)
Chargeable gain	1,400

The cost of cleaning and repairs is not capital expenditure. As the brooch was both bought and sold for more than £6,000, the chattel rules do not apply.

26   A   Erwin sold a painting at auction and received £6,100 after deducting auctioneers fees of £200. The painting had originally cost him £3,500 – Chargeable

          This is a disposal of a non wasting chattel with gross sale proceeds of more than £6,000, so chargeable.

       C   Eryk received £5,900 for jewellery that he sold. The jewellery originally cost him £5,900 plus auctioneers fees of £200 – Chargeable

          The total cost of acquiring the jewellery was more than £6,000 (£5,900 + £200) so the disposal is chargeable.

27   B   £500

          Gain is (£6,300 – £4,000) = £2,300 but restricted to

          (Gross sale proceeds – £6,000) × 5/3 = (£6,300 – £6,000) × 5/3 = £500

28   A   £0

          Both gross sale proceeds and cost are less than £6,000 so exempt.

29   A   An antique diamond necklace worth £3,000 (cost £2,500)

       E   Shares held in an ISA

30   A   Legal fees on purchase

       B   Purchase price

       D   Cost of building garage

31   A   Gain of £3,600 on the sale of goodwill in her ice cream van business – Chargeable gain

       D   Loss of £2,000 on the sale of a diamond necklace which had cost £4,000 – Exempt

       Goodwill is not a chattel, so cannot be exempt under the £6,000 rule.

       The diamond necklace is a chattel. Gross sale proceeds and cost were less than £6,000

32   C   A gain of £4,200 on the sale of his 10 year old racehorse – decrease

          The gain arising on the sale of the race horse is exempt.

       D   Auctioneer's fees of £500 on sale – no effect

       This question is from the sample paper issued by ICAEW.

33   A   £36,040

	£
Sale proceeds	500,000
Less legal fees	(25,000)
Net sale proceeds	475,000
Less original cost	(280,000)
Chargeable gain	195,000
Less annual exempt amount	(11,300)
Taxable gain	183,700

CGT liability	
(£33,500 – £26,500) £7,000 × 10%	700
(£183,700 – £7,000) × 20%	35,340
	36,040

34   A   £4,720

	£
Sale proceeds	56,000
Less auctioneer's fees	(1,100)
Net sale proceeds	54,900
Less MV on death	(20,000)
Chargeable gain	34,900
Less annual exempt amount	(11,300)
Taxable gain	23,600

CGT liability	
£23,600 × 20%	4,720

35   B   Gain of £13,000 on the shares in an ISA – Exempt

Gains on shares held in an ISA are exempt.

C   Loss of £3,000 on shares which had cost £5,000 – Allowable capital loss

Shares are not chattels and so not subject to the chattels exemption where gross sale proceeds and cost are less than £6,000

36   C   Sale for £5,000 of the goodwill of a trading business by Jack.

Goodwill is not a chattel so not subject to the exemption where gross sales proceeds and cost are less than £6,000.

Cash, cars and premium bonds are all exempt assets.

37   D   £5,580

	£
Sale proceeds	50,200
Less cost plus frame (£8,000 + £2,000)	(10,000)
Chargeable gain	40,200
Less annual exempt amount	(11,300)
Taxable gain	28,900

CGT liability	
(£33,500 – £31,500) £2,000 × 10%	200
(£28,900 – £2,000) × 20%	5,380
	5,580

38   B   £94,983

	£
Sale proceeds	1,250,400
Less estate agents' fees	(120,000)
Net sale proceeds	1,130,400
Less original cost	(642,000)
Chargeable gain	488,400
Less annual exempt amount	(11,300)
Taxable gain	477,100
CGT liability	
(£33,500 – £29,130) £4,370 × 10%	437
(477,100 – £4,370) × 20%	94,546
	94,983

This question is from the sample paper issued by ICAEW.

Chapter 10: Corporation tax

1   D   0.571

As this is a disposal by a company, indexation runs from the date of acquisition to the date of disposal. For enhancement expenditure, such as an extension, indexation runs from the date of expenditure to the date of disposal. Indexation therefore runs from December 2001 to September 2017:

(262.4 – 173.4)/173.4 = 0.571 (round to 3 decimal places)

2   B   £(12,400)

As a non-wasting asset, the chattel rules apply. As it was sold at a loss, actual proceeds are substituted by deemed proceeds of £6,000 to restrict the loss. No indexation is available as it cannot augment a loss.

	£
Deemed proceeds	6,000
Less selling fees	(400)
Net sale proceeds	5,600
Less cost	(18,000)
Loss	(12,400)

3   B   Gain of £24,000 on the disposal of a rare African snake which had not been used in the business – Exempt

The snake is a wasting asset which is an exempt asset unless it was used in the business and was eligible for capital allowances.

C   Gain of £1,100 on the sale of an antique chair. The chair originally cost £5,000 – Chargeable gain

The chair is a non-wasting asset which is chargeable. As it was not bought and sold for less than £6,000 (sales proceeds must exceed £6,000 for the level of gain), it is chargeable subject to the chattel rules.

4   Unindexed gain £ 1,604,071

	£
Sale proceeds	2,125,000
Less disposal costs	(24,969)
Net sale proceeds	2,100,031
Less cost + acquisition costs (£432,000 + £3,000 + £12,960)	(447,960)
Less enhancement expenditure	(48,000)
Unindexed gain	1,604,071

5   A   £62,520

For companies, indexation runs from the date of acquisition to the date of disposal. The indexation factor must be rounded to three decimal places.

$$\frac{273.8 - 134.1}{134.1} = 1.042 \times £60,000 = £62,520$$

This question is from the sample paper issued by ICAEW.

6   D   £152,900

	£
Sale proceeds	425,000
Cost	(150,000)
Indexation (0.814 × £150,000)	(122,100)
Chargeable gain	152,900

No annual exempt amount for companies.

7   D   Individuals will have a chargeable gain on disposal of goodwill from their business

Goodwill is a chargeable asset for individuals (but not for companies).

8   C   £3,040

Companies pay corporation tax on gains (at 19%). Companies do not have an annual exempt amount.

19% × £16,000 = £3,040

9   B   1 July 2017 – 31 December 2017

Lettuce Ltd's first accounting period commences when it first acquires a source of income or begins to trade, whichever is earlier. In this case opening a building society account means it has acquired a source of income. This first accounting period will, in this case, end when it commences to trade.

Its second accounting period will run from the next day to, in this case, the end of its period of account, ie, 1 January 2018 to 30 September 2018. Its third accounting period onwards will be the same as its periods of account.

10   A   A company which is centrally managed and controlled in the UK will always be liable to UK corporation tax on its worldwide profits **is true**.

A company which is incorporated in the UK will always be liable to UK corporation tax on its worldwide profits; it does not matter where its central management and control is exercised.

A company which is incorporated abroad and centrally managed and controlled abroad will **never** be liable to UK corporation tax on its worldwide profits.

A company which is incorporated abroad will never be liable to UK corporation tax on its worldwide profits **as long as it is also centrally managed and controlled abroad**.

This question is from the sample paper issued by ICAEW.

11   D   1 August 2017 – 31 January 2018

Airedale Ltd's first accounting period commences when it first acquires a source of income or begins to trade, whichever is earlier. In this case opening a building society account means it has acquired a source of income. This first accounting period will, in this case, end when it commences to trade. Its first accounting period is 1 August 2017 – 31 January 2018.

Its second accounting period will run from the next day to, in this case, the end of its period of account ie, 1 February 2018 to 30 September 2018.

Its third accounting period onwards will be the same as its periods of account.

12   Papillon Ltd's corporation tax liability £ | 66,500 |

Papillon's corporation tax liability is:

£350,000 × 19% = £66,500.

13   B   Loss on sale of two cars – Exempt

D   Gain on sale of an investment property – Chargeable gain

This question is from the sample paper issued by ICAEW.

14   Unindexed gain £ | 119,900 |

	£
Proceeds	312,000
Less: cost	(165,000)
fees (£2,450 + £1,650)	(4,100)
Extension	(23,000)
Unindexed gain	119,900

The repair is not enhancement expenditure.

15   Corporation tax payable £ | 206,834 |

£1,088,600 × 19% = £206,834

16   B   1 February 2016 to 31 January 2017

        A corporation tax accounting period cannot exceed 12 months in length.

This question is from the sample paper issued by ICAEW.

17   Corporation tax payable £ | 49,400 |

	Y/e 31 December 2017 £
Taxable total profits	260,000
Corporation tax payable:	
£260,000 × 19%	49,400

Chapter 11: Value added tax

1   B   8 May

The time the goods are made available – invoice not issued within 14 days.

2   D   Entertaining costs of UK business customers

Van accessories – business assets – OK.

Partitioning and motor cycle – business assets – OK.

Entertaining – statutory disallowance of input tax except for entertaining employees and foreign customers.

3   A   Demonstrate to HMRC that he intends to make either zero or standard-rated supplies or both.

A person not required to be registered must be registered if he so requests and if HMRC is satisfied that he makes taxable supplies (standard and/or zero-rated) or is carrying on a business and intends to make taxable supplies.

4   C   He must register, based on turnover of standard and zero-rated supplies, which exceed £85,000.

Registration limit is in relation to taxable supplies, defined as standard and zero-rated supplies (and reduced rate supplies if any).

5   D   £200

The eventual VAT paid is £1,000 @ 20% because Bronco Ltd does not qualify for any settlement discounts.

6   B   30 March 2018

First 12-month period in which £85,000 limit exceeded is y/e 28 February 2018.
Total = £85,100

Notification is required 30 days after the end of month in which limit is exceeded, ie, 30 March 2018.

7   B   £5,425

VAT may be reclaimed on vehicles (new or second-hand) other than cars used privately.

	£
On van ($£9,450 \times \frac{1}{6}$)	1,575
On lorry ($£23,100 \times \frac{1}{6}$)	3,850
	5,425

8   A   The debtor does not need to be formally insolvent.

9   A   1 February

The basic tax point is the date that the goods are dispatched to Tariq, ie, 8 February.

However, where the supplier issues an invoice or receives payment before the basic tax point, the earlier date becomes the actual tax point. So in this case as both the invoice and the payment occur before the basic tax point, the earlier of these two dates becomes the actual tax point, ie, 1 February when the invoice is issued.

10   B   £400.00

A gift of business assets is a deemed supply for VAT purposes, unless it is a trade sample or the cost of gifts made to the same person in a 12-month period does not exceed £50.

The gift of the laptop is therefore a deemed supply. The value of the supply is the VAT exclusive cost Quentin would have had to pay at the time of the supply to replace the laptop, ie, £2,000.

The output VAT to be accounted for by Quentin is £2,000 × 20% = 400.00

11   B   Two

A 'person' for VAT purposes includes an individual sole trader, partnership, limited company, club, association or charity. A person's registration covers all of his business activities, however diverse. It is the 'person' who is registered, not the business.

Therefore, Valerie will register as a sole trader (with two businesses) and the partnership will have a separate registration.

12   C   £302.40

VAT is calculated after both trade discount and cash discounts, as payment is made within the specified time period. Therefore VAT on invoice is £302.40 (£1,512 @ 20%).

13   A   4 May

As the payment is received before the basic tax point date (BTPD) ie, dispatch, the date of payment becomes the actual tax point date. It is worth noting here that the invoice was issued within 14 days of the BTPD and this would then normally have become the tax point unless payment is made before the invoice date.

14   B   29 June 2017 to notify HMRC

     D   31 May 2017 to start charging VAT

Priscilla must notify HMRC by the end of the 30-day period for which it is believed the threshold will be exceeded. Under the future prospects test registration takes effect from the beginning of the 30-day period.

15   C   Use of car for her wedding only

The gift of services (to the cousin or anyone else) is specifically not a taxable supply. As opposed to a gift of goods which is a deemed supply.

The private use of goods owned by a business and the private use of services, supplied to the business, by the owner are taxable supplies.

16   C   2 April

As an invoice is issued within fourteen days of the basic tax point ie, dispatch, the date on which the invoice is issued becomes the actual tax point. The end of the quarter does not affect this.

17   C   £10,310

	£
Invoice total including VAT	10,470
Less vehicle excise duty	(160)
	10,310

VAT on motor cars with any amount of private use is irrecoverable; it is therefore included in the capital cost for capital allowance purposes.

This question is from the sample paper issued by ICAEW.

18   B   A tax invoice is held

To be recoverable the goods or services must be used for business purposes and the input VAT must be supported by a VAT invoice.

19 C £80

VAT in respect of lunches on business trips is recoverable (£480 × $\frac{1}{6}$ = £80)

20 A Both businesses

A 'person' for VAT purposes includes an individual sole trader, partnership, limited company, club, association or charity. A person's registration covers all of his or her business activities, however diverse. It is the 'person' who is registered, not the business.

Therefore, Parminder will register as a sole trader with two businesses and will have to charge VAT to the customers of both businesses.

21 B 2 March to notify HMRC

D 1 February to start charging VAT

Sheep plc must notify HMRC by the end of the 30-day period for which it is believed the threshold will be exceeded, ie, by 2 March. Under the future prospects test registration takes effect from the beginning of the 30-day period.

22 C Deregistration will be effective immediately and must be notified by 30 March 2018

Cow plc must deregister as it is no longer making taxable supplies. A wholly exempt trader cannot be registered for VAT. The registration will be effective immediately but Cow plc has 30 days in which to notify HMRC, ie, by 30 March.

23 B £165.67

VAT collected = (£400 × 20%) + (£514 × $\frac{1}{6}$) = £165.67.

24 What is the correct amount of output VAT paid by Ferdinand overall?   £ [192]

£1,000 × 96% × 20% = £192

VAT is calculated on the price of the supply less the maximum discount as the discount is taken up here.

25 A UK client entertaining

E Company car for employee use which is a taxable benefit for income tax purposes

The VAT on UK client entertaining is never recoverable. The VAT on a company car with private use by an employee is also irrecoverable. For the car to qualify as a taxable benefit there must be private use.

The VAT on fuel in company pool cars is recoverable. VAT on capital purchases for business use is always recoverable. As a pre-registration purchase, it must still be owned at registration and have been purchased within four years pre registration. VAT on gifts of goods to customers is recoverable although output VAT must be charged as a deemed supply.

26 C 30 July 2018

Wayne must register for VAT once his taxable turnover for the prior 12 months exceeds the VAT registration threshold. This happens during the month to 30 June 2018 when his turnover reaches £85,600. He is therefore liable to notify his liability by 30 July 2018.

27 A £770

VAT may be recovered on all three items. The VAT on the van may be recovered as it is still held in the business at the time of registration and was purchased within four years of registration. The same applies to the stock of spare parts. The invoice for accountancy services is dated no more than six months before the date of registration and is therefore also recoverable.

28 B VAT is chargeable on zero-rated supplies, at 0%.

A trader who is wholly exempt may not register for VAT. VAT at the standard rate is charged at 20%. A trader making taxable supplies may voluntarily register for VAT even where taxable supplies are below the VAT registration threshold.

29 A 30 December 2017

As Michael's turnover is £85,200 for the 12 months ended 30 November 2017, he must notify HMRC within 30 days, ie, by 30 December 2017.

30 C Miranda may choose to deregister but would then need to pay output VAT on the deemed supply of stock and capital items still held at deregistration if the output VAT exceeds £1,000.

As Miranda's taxable supplies are now below the registration threshold and her forecast taxable turnover is below the deregistration threshold, she may choose to deregister. She may remain registered if she prefers, as she still makes some taxable supplies.

On deregistration, there is a deemed supply of trade stock and capital items on which VAT has previously been recovered. Output VAT is payable on this deemed supply subject to it being greater than £1,000.

31 C Gifts of services worth £100 to a customer.

Gifts of services are never a deemed supply. Gifts of business assets worth less than £50 per annum per recipient are not a deemed supply.

32 A £256

In order to recover input VAT on purchases the item must be for business purposes and be supported by a valid VAT invoice. Only the VAT on the office stationery is therefore recoverable.

33 B A gift of business services is not a taxable supply.

Where discounts are available, the overall amount of VAT should be calculated based on discounts actually taken up, not those offered.

The value of the supply of a business asset used for private purposes is the cost to the taxable person of providing the asset.

Input VAT is irrecoverable if there is any element of private use of the car.

34 D 31 March 2018

In order to recover output VAT on an unpaid invoice, the debt must be more than six months old and the debt must have been written off in the accounts. Six months from the due date of payment of 31 August 2017 is 28 February 2018. However, as the debt is not written off in Flight plc's accounts until 31 March 2018, that becomes the earliest date that Flight plc could make a claim to recover the unpaid output VAT.

35 A 1 September

The basic tax point is the date that the goods are dispatched to Sunil, ie, 8 September.

However, where the supplier issues an invoice before the basic tax point, ie, on 1 September, this date becomes the actual tax point.

36 C 1 November

Basic tax point for goods on sale or return is the adoption date (maximum of 12 months later) – so 1 November. Invoice date is more than 14 days later so actual tax point is the basic tax point.

37 C 29 October

Basic tax point is the date the goods are made available to the customer (18 October). However actual tax point is invoice date (29 October) as it is less than 14 days after the basic tax point.

38 C Disco Ltd must be making or intending to make some taxable supplies.

The alternative answers are incorrect because:
The company can register if it makes a mixture of taxable and exempt supplies.
It is advantageous to register if expecting to be in a repayment position but it is not required.

The company does not have to be expecting to exceed the VAT threshold.

39 B The company is required to notify HMRC of its liability to register by 30 November 2017

F Registration takes effect from 1 December 2017

Under the historic turnover test, a trader must notify HMRC within 30 days of the end of the month in which the threshold was exceeded. Registration is effective from the first of the month after the end of the month following the threshold being exceeded.

40 C No, based on taxable supplies of normal trading

Include taxable supplies to determine whether the threshold is exceeded, but exclude supplies of capital assets.

41 B £244

	£
Accommodation	64
Laptop (business use)	180
	244

The meals are part of salary hence outside the scope. The laptop is provided as part of an employee's remuneration package and is a valid expense of the business. Therefore there is no restriction for private use.

42 B £1,680

VAT is irrecoverable on motor cars where there is private use, hence recoverable on the van only.

$(1/6 \times £10,080) = £1,680$

43 B A period of six months has elapsed since the goods were supplied – Incorrect

C Tax on the supply has been accounted for and paid – Correct

F The bad debt claim must be made within six years of becoming eligible for relief – Incorrect

A period of six months must have elapsed since the **due date for payment**.

The bad debt claim must be made within **four** years of becoming eligible for relief.

44 B £1,152

Maximum discount obtained 10% = £5,760 × 20% = £1,152

45 A 3 April

If payment is received before the basic tax point, payment date is the actual tax point.

46 B Steve, who is registered for VAT, runs a plant hire company. In the quarter ended 31 March 2018 he let his brother use a digger at no charge – Not taxable

A gift of services is not a taxable supply.

C In the quarter to 30 June 2018 he used the same digger to help dig the foundations for the extension being built onto his house – Taxable

Goods owned by a business and temporarily used by the owner are a taxable supply.

47 A £25,380

Input tax is not recoverable on cars and accessories fitted when supplied, where the car is not used 100% for business.

48 D £100.00

VAT-exclusive price payable by the person supplying the asset to purchase an identical replacement (ie, at cost).

49 Wood Ltd still owes £5,000 from an invoice issued on 30 June 2017. Gertrude still believes that the amount will be paid in full and so it has not been written off in the accounts.

B Bad debt relief cannot be claimed

Wood Ltd – not written off so not reclaimable.

Trees Ltd owes £2,000 from an invoice issued on 15 September 2017. Gertrude does not expect payment of this and has written it off in the accounts.

D Bad debt relief cannot be claimed

Trees Ltd – not yet six months since **payment** due (15 October 2017).

50 A Only the goods used in Jacob's house are a taxable supply

51 B A business making £48,000 of standard-rated supplies and £38,000 of exempt supplies is required to VAT register – Incorrect

VAT registration is required if **taxable** turnover exceeds £85,000 ie, exclude exempt turnover.

C A business making £86,000 of zero-rated supplies only does not have to become VAT registered – Correct

A business making purely zero-rated supplies can apply for exemption from registration.

52 C 1 March 2018

From the first day after the end of the month following the cumulative turnover exceeding £85,000.

It exceeds the limit at the end of January 2018 (5 × £4,900) + (6 × £7,700) + £14,400 = £85,100. So VAT registered from 1 March 2018.

53 It must notify HMRC of its liability to VAT register by

B 30 January 2018

The company's VAT registration is effective from

D 1 January 2018

Future prospects rule – 30 days to notify – 30 January 2018

– Immediate liability to charge VAT – 1 January 2018

54 A £12.67

C Payable by Maddie

Maddie is liable for the VAT that should have been paid on the sale. The consideration received by Maddie is deemed to be VAT-inclusive.

Therefore the amount of output VAT payable is £76 × 1/6 = £12.67

55 B Exempt supplies – Do not include

D Supply of surplus office machinery – Do not include

56 C Machine with no VAT invoice – not recoverable

F Purchase of car – not recoverable

This question is from the sample paper issued by ICAEW.

57 B £192 – Quarter to 28 February 2018

E £1,725 – Quarter to 31 May 2018

58 A Amount of VAT payable – £16.67

C VAT is payable by David

This question is from the sample paper issued by the ICAEW.

59 B A trader can voluntarily register for VAT if he makes only zero-rated supplies.

C A trader making both zero-rated and standard-rated supplies is required to register only if the level of taxable supplies exceeds the VAT registration limit.

This question is from the sample paper issued by ICAEW.

60 Output VAT £ 5,912

Output VAT

£29,560 × 20% = £5,912

This question is from the sample paper issued by ICAEW.

61 Input VAT £ 3,030

£(900 + 2,130)

This question is from the sample paper issued by ICAEW.

62 C 30 December 2017

Turnover	£
January to August (£6,150 × 8)	49,200
September/October	23,000
November	13,000
	85,200

The VAT registration limit is therefore exceeded at the end of November.

This question is from the sample paper issued by ICAEW.

63 C Output VAT £ 63.17

The VAT-inclusive quarterly scale rate for a car with CO_2 emissions between 185g/km and 189g/km is £379. £379 × 1/6 = £63.17

Chapter 12: Value added tax – further aspects

1   C   7 May 2018

    F   7 May 2018

       A VAT return is filed electronically and due seven days after the end of the month following the end of the return period. Payment must also be made electronically and the deadline is the same.

2   D   Two payments of £125,000 each and a balancing payment of £650,000

       A trader with an annual VAT liability in excess of £2.3 million is known as a 'substantial trader' and is required to make payments on account (POA) during each quarter. The POA are made in months 2 and 3 of each quarter with a balancing payment made one month after the quarter end. The payments required from Cornflower plc are:

	£
28 February 2018 = 1/24 × £3,000,000	125,000
31 March 2018 = 1/24 × £3,000,000	125,000
30 April 2018 = balancing payment due for the quarter ended 31 March 2018	650,000
	900,000

3   C   £250

       If a simplified VAT invoice is to be issued, the maximum consideration permitted is £250.

4   A   A VAT invoice must be issued to all taxable and non-taxable customers.

       A VAT invoice must be issued to all taxable customers, but it is not necessary to issue a VAT invoice to non-taxable customers, although an invoice often is issued in practice.

    C   A simplified invoice may be issued if the VAT-inclusive sale proceeds are less than £500.

       A simplified invoice may be issued if the VAT-inclusive sale proceeds are not more than £250.

5   D   She pays her VAT in nine monthly instalments starting in April 2017 with a balancing payment and the return submitted by 28 February 2018.

6   D   £4,500 by 31 May 2018

       Nine payments on account equal to 1/10 of the previous year's VAT liability are made. Any balancing payment and the VAT return are due two months after the end of the year.

7   D   Both

       Taxable persons must keep records of all transactions to support both the output VAT charged and the claim for recoverable input VAT.

8   B   £1,350,000

       The annual accounting scheme is available if the value of taxable supplies (excluding VAT and supplies of capital items) does not exceed £1,350,000.

9   C   Each payment on account is 1/24 of the total VAT liability of the previous year.

       Under the VAT payment on accounts scheme, large traders (VAT annual liability > £2.3 million) make monthly payments on account. Within each quarter, VAT equivalent to 1/24 of the previous year's VAT liability is payable in months 2 and 3. One month after the end of each quarter the balance, if any, for that quarter is payable. Thus for a trader with a December year end payments will be made from January to December. The payment for January will relate to the previous quarter and the other 11 payments will relate to the current year. The seven day extension does not apply to the payments on account scheme.

10　B　Businesses operating the flat rate scheme apply their sector percentage to total (both taxable and exempt) VAT inclusive turnover.

　　C　HMRC may grant exemption from registration to zero-rated traders that have negligible amounts of input VAT.

　　　　Businesses with an annual VAT liability in excess of £2.3 million must join the VAT payments on account scheme.

　　　　The main advantage of the annual accounting scheme is the need to only file one annual VAT return.

　　　　Businesses operating the cash accounting scheme may also join the annual accounting scheme and vice versa.

11　C　The scheme is advantageous for businesses making only zero-rated supplies

　　E　Businesses in the scheme must leave if taxable supplies in the previous 12 months exceed £1.35 million.

　　　　Businesses making zero rated supplies only reclaim input tax – the reclaim will not be sooner using cash accounting.

　　　　A business must leave the cash accounting scheme if taxable supplies in the previous 12 months exceed £1.6 million.

12　A trader may join the annual accounting scheme where the taxable turnover in the following year is not expected to exceed £ ⌐1,350,000⌐

13　B　£550,000

　　　　Monthly instalments £3m/24 = £125,000

　　　　Balance due one month after quarter end = £(800,000 – 125,000 – 125,000) = £550,000

14　B　Automatic bad debt relief is given.

　　　　This is a feature of the cash accounting scheme.

15　A　Businesses calculate VAT due as a flat rate percentage of their VAT exclusive turnover.

　　　　The VAT is calculated on the VAT **inclusive** turnover.

16　D　£1,122

　　　　The flat rate percentage is applied to the total (both taxable and exempt) turnover of the business inclusive of VAT, ie, £8,500 × 1.20 × 11% = £1,122.

17　C　£2,008

　　　　As Florence Ltd operates the cash accounting scheme its tax point is the date of payment to suppliers or the date of receipt of payment from customers. Hence any input tax which is paid in the quarter is also recoverable in the quarter. VAT on the artwork and the marketing literature is therefore recoverable in this quarter. VAT on the spare machinery parts will be recovered in the next quarter.

18　D　4 June

　　　　Since Gordon is a member of the cash accounting scheme output VAT is accounted for when the payment is received from the customer.

　　This question is from the sample paper issued by ICAEW.

19　D　£1,632

　　　　Within the flat rate scheme, output VAT is calculated as the relevant business % × VAT inclusive turnover. There is no recovery of input VAT. Therefore Tony's VAT payable to HMRC is £17,000 × 1.20 × 8% = £1,632.

20　B　A trader using the flat rate scheme may also be authorised to use the annual accounting scheme.

　　D　Where a customer requires an invoice, a flat rate trader who makes wholly standard-rated supplies will issue a VAT invoice showing 20% output tax.

　　This question is from the sample paper issued by ICAEW.

21　B　Automatic bad debt relief is given

　　C　Output VAT is accounted for when cash is received from the customer

　　This question is from the sample paper issued by ICAEW.

22　B　16.5% of VAT inclusive turnover.

Chapter 13: Administration of tax

1   A   5 October 2017

A taxpayer is required to notify HMRC of the need to complete a self-assessment return by 5 October following the tax year in which a new source of income is acquired. As Camilla commenced to trade in 2016/17 she is required to notify by 5 October 2017.

This question is from the sample paper issued by ICAEW.

2   C   15 March 2019

A taxpayer who wishes to submit a tax return online must do so by the later of 31 January following the tax year end and three months from the date the return was issued.

3   A   Andrew may file a short tax return

    C   Andrew may file a short tax return

A taxpayer who is an employee but not a director, a sole trader with a turnover of less than £83,000 per annum or a pensioner is not required to submit a full tax return each year. The taxpayer may however, decide to continue to submit a full tax return in any event. This is voluntary and not a requirement unless the taxpayer is sent a full return by HMRC or wants to submit online.

4   B   31 January 2024

    C   31 January 2020

Because he has a business, Edward must keep records (of whatever nature) for his 2017/18 tax return until 31 January 2024. Records where a taxpayer has a business must be kept for five years from the 31 January following the end of the tax year to which they relate.

Where a taxpayer is not in business (ie, the records are purely personal), the records must be kept for one year from the 31 January following the end of the tax year to which they relate, ie, 31 January 2020.

5   C   31 January 2019

A return may be amended for any reason within 12 months of when the return should have been filed, not when it was actually filed. A return relating to 2016/17 should have been filed by 31 January 2018. The amendment must therefore be made by 31 January 2019.

6   B   31 January 2018, 31 July 2018 and 31 January 2019

A sole trader who is not in his first year is required to make payments on account. Eugenie must therefore make payments on account on 31 January in the tax year and 31 July following the tax year end. A final balancing payment is made on 31 January following the tax year end.

7   Payment on account   £ [5,500]

Harry's payments on account (POA) for 2017/18 will be half of the income tax and class 4 NICs paid under self assessment in 2016/17:

	£
Income tax liability for 2016/17	15,000
Less income tax deducted at source	(6,000)
	9,000
Plus NIC class 4 for 2016/17	2,000
	11,000
× 50%	5,500

Payments on account are not due in respect of capital gains tax.

8 C All of the payments were made late and will be liable to interest from the due date to the day before payment but only the balancing payment is liable to a penalty at 5%

Sophie's payments should have been made on 31 January 2018, 31 July 2018 and 31 January 2019. They were all late and will be liable to interest from the due date to the day before payment. In addition the balancing payment is potentially liable to a penalty. Where it is paid more than 30 days late (the penalty date), the penalty is 5%. Where it is paid more than six months after the payment due date, there is a further penalty of 5%.

9 C 5 October 2018

A taxpayer is required to notify HMRC of the need to complete a self assessment return by 5 October following the tax year in which a new source of income is acquired. As Albert commenced to trade in 2017/18 he is required to notify by 5 October 2018.

10 D 31 January 2024 – five years after the 31 January following 2017/18 (five years after 31 January 2019)

11 A By 30 November 2018 if he wants HMRC to calculate his tax

  E By 31 January 2019 if he wants to file online

If HMRC is to calculate the tax liability, the normal due date for filing the tax return is 31 October following the end of the tax year.

However, where the notice to make a return is issued after 31 July following the end of the tax year, the deadline is extended to three months after the issue of the notice if the taxpayer calculates their own tax liability, or the deadline is extended by two months after the issue of the notice if HMRC are to calculate the tax, ie, 30 November 2018 in this case.

If the taxpayer is to file online, the normal due date for filing the tax return is 31 January following the end of the tax year.

Where the notice to make a return is issued after 31 October following the end of the tax year, the deadline is extended to three months after the issue of the notice – not relevant in this case.

12 A Elaine can amend her tax return on 15 December 2019.

  C Elaine can make a claim for overpayment relief because there is an error in her return on 31 December 2021.

A taxpayer can amend his/her tax return any time before 12 months after 31 January following the tax year, ie, before 31 January 2020 for a 2017/18 return issued on 6 May 2018. Elaine can therefore amend her tax return on 15 December 2019.

HMRC can correct any obvious errors or mistakes in a taxpayer's tax return within nine months of the date the return is filed, ie, 1 September 2019 for a return filed on 1 December 2018. HMRC cannot therefore correct an arithmetical error in Elaine's return on 29 September 2019.

A taxpayer can make a claim for overpayment relief within four years of the end of the tax year, ie, before 5 April 2022 for 2017/18. Elaine can therefore make a claim on 31 December 2021 that there is an error in her return.

HMRC can give notice of an enquiry into a return until 12 months after the actual filing date of the return ie, 12 months after 1 December 2018. Therefore notice cannot be given on 20 December 2019.

13 If HMRC wishes to collect the unpaid tax, it must raise an assessment by 5 April ｜ 2022 ｜

Where the taxpayer has made an incomplete disclosure of facts in his tax return, which is not due to careless or deliberate behaviour, HMRC has until four years after the end of the tax year to raise a discovery assessment, ie, 5 April 2022 for 2017/18.

14   A   £0

Tax payable for 2016/17

	£
Total tax liability	28,450
Paid at source	(23,400)
Balance payable under self assessment	5,050

The balance payable by self assessment re 2016/17 is 17.75% (£5,050 ÷ £28,450) of the total income tax liability for that year. As this is less than 20% of the total tax liability, payments on account are not required in 2017/18.

Therefore no payment on account of Harriet's 2017/18 tax liability should have been paid on 31 July 2018.

15   On 31 January 2018, to avoid interest charges, Ivan should have paid tax of £ ⎡ 9,350 ⎤

The tax due on 31 January 2018 is calculated as follows.

	£	£
Balancing payment for 2016/17		
Total tax liability	15,500	
Class 4 NICs	3,200	
Paid under PAYE	(3,800)	
Tax paid by self assessment	14,900	
Payments on account	(13,000)	
		1,900
Payment on account for 2017/18		
50% of tax paid by self assessment for 2016/17 (50% × £14,900)		7,450
Tax due on 31 January 2018		9,350

16   C   £6,600

Tax payable for 2016/17

	£	£
Total income tax liability	18,200	
Paid under PAYE	(5,000)	
Balance paid by self assessment	13,200	
Payment on account for 2017/18 due 31 July 2018		
50% of tax paid by self assessment for 2016/17 (50% × £13,200)		6,600

Payments on account are not required in respect of capital gains tax. Capital gains tax is settled via one payment on 31 January following the end of the tax year.

17   B   £190

A penalty of 5% of the tax overdue is payable where income tax, Class 4 NICs and capital gains tax are paid more than 30 days after the due date. Penalties do not, however, apply to payments on account.

Where the tax is still outstanding six months after the payment due date a further 5% of the tax overdue is charged.

The balancing payment for income tax paid late is £1,500 (£9,500 – £8,000 POA) and the capital gains tax of £2,300 is also paid late.

Kurt will therefore be liable for a penalty of £190, being 5% of the total amount paid late of £3,800 (£1,500 + £2,300), which was due on 31 January 2018.

This question is from the sample paper issued by ICAEW.

18 B   Interest will run on the additional liability of £1,500 from 1 April 2018 to 14 May 2018 – False

Interest runs from the due filing date (31 January 2018 for 2016/17) until the day before the tax is paid. The first statement is therefore not true.

C   A late payment penalty of £75 is payable by Martha – True

A penalty of £75, being 5% of £1,500, will apply to the additional tax arising. The second statement is therefore true.

19 B   An appeal against a discovery assessment must be made in writing within a calendar month of the date of the assessment – False

An appeal against a discovery assessment must be made in writing within 30 days of the date of the assessment. Therefore the statement is not true.

D   The taxpayer must first apply for an internal review before making an appeal to the First-tier Tribunal – False

An internal review is optional.

E   A taxpayer can appeal against and apply to postpone the tax due under an assessment raised as a result of an enquiry into a tax return – True

This question is from the sample paper issued by ICAEW.

20 B   5 October 2018

Where HMRC does not issue a tax return it must be notified of chargeable gains arising by 5 October following the end of the tax year in which the gain arose.

21 C   5 April 2038

HMRC may raise a discovery assessment where full disclosure has not been made either due to negligence or fraud at any time up until 20 years after the end of the tax year.

22 B   Before the debt is recovered, there will be a period when Fred can object to the recovery.

D   HMRC must be satisfied that Fred is aware that the sum is due.

HMRC can recover the debt in this way if it is at least £1,000.

Fred must be left with at least £5,000 in his accounts after the debt recovery.

23 A   £0

Tax payable for 2016/17

	£
Total income tax liability	23,200
Paid under PAYE	(19,000)
Balance payable under self assessment	4,200

The balance payable by self assessment re 2016/17 is 18.1% (£4,200 ÷ £23,200) of the total income tax liability for that year. As this is less than 20% of the total tax liability, payments on account are not required in 2017/18.

Payments on account are not required in respect of capital gains tax. Capital gains tax is settled via one payment on the 31 January following the end of the tax year.

Therefore no payment on account of Greg's 2017/18 liability should have been paid on 31 July 2018.

24 Harold is due to make a payment on 31 July 2018. To minimise any interest charges you would
advise that he makes a payment on that date of £ [9,700]

Tax payable for 2016/17

	£
Total income tax liability	12,100
Class 4 NIC	3,400
Tax deducted at source	(300)
Balance payable under self assessment	15,200

Two equal payments on account of 50% of the previous year's tax paid by self assessment are due
on 31 January 2018 and 31 July 2018 in respect of 2017/18.

By 31 July 2018 Harold should have paid 100% of the previous year's tax due by self assessment, ie,
£15,200. As he has only paid £5,500 to date he should pay the balance of £9,700 on 31 July 2018
in order to minimise any interest charges.

25 B   £100

Ingrid should have submitted her 2016/17 tax return on 31 January 2018. A fixed penalty of
£100 is due as it was submitted less than three months late.

The second payment on account was paid on 31 August 2017. The payment was due on
31 July 2017; however, no penalties are due on late payments on account.

Ingrid paid the final balancing payment for 2016/17 on 15 February 2018, 15 days late.
Interest will be due but no penalty is due as the tax was not outstanding more than 30 days
after the due date.

26 She wants HMRC to calculate her tax liability

B   31 January 2019

The normal due date for filing a tax return where HMRC is to compute the liability is
31 October following the end of the tax year. However, where the notice to make a return is
issued after 31 July following the end of the tax year, the deadline is extended to two months
after the issue of the notice if HMRC are to calculate the tax liability, ie, 31 January 2019.

She intends to calculate her own tax liability

F   28 February 2019

The due date for filing a tax return where the taxpayer is to compute the liability is the later of
31 October following the end of the tax year or three months after the issue of the notice, ie,
28 February 2019.

This question is from the sample paper issued by ICAEW.

27 A   31 January 2019

The balancing payment is due by 31 January 2019.

F   HMRC may amend the return until 10 June 2019.

This question is from the sample paper issued by ICAEW.

28 B   19 April 2017

D   6 July 2017

PAYE is payable 14 days after the end of each tax month. The last month of the tax year ends
on 5 April 2017. It is therefore due by 19 April 2017.

P11D forms are due to be submitted to both HMRC and given to the employees by 6 July
following the tax year end.

29 B   Form issued when an employee leaves employment

    D   End of year summary of tax and NICs per employee to be issued to each employee

        An end of year summary of tax and NICs deducted in the year per employee to be issued to each employee is a P60.

30 A   30% potential lost revenue

    C   £300 per return

        The fine for filing an incorrect P11D, with careless inaccuracies is 30% of potential lost revenue. The initial penalty for filing a late P11D is £300 per return.

31 B   31 May

32 A   P11D – 6 July 2018

    D   P60 – 31 May 2018

        This question is from the sample paper issued by ICAEW.

33 C   31 December 2020

        A claim for 'overpayment relief' must be made within four years of the end of the accounting period.

34 A   31 August 2018

        HMRC has the right to amend a corporation return for obvious errors or omissions for nine months from the date the return is actually filed, ie, from 30 November 2017.

35 D   30 April 2019

        Where a return is filed late, HMRC has the right to give notice of its intention to conduct an enquiry into a return for 12 months from the next quarter date of actual submission. The quarter dates are 31 January, 30 April, 31 July, and 31 October. The return should have been filed within 12 months of the period of account end, ie, by 31 December 2017. As Azure plc filed its return late on 28 February 2018, the next quarter date is 30 April 2018, so the anniversary of that date is 30 April 2019.

36 B   £200

    C   10% of tax unpaid at 28 February 2018

        The return should have been filed within 12 months of the period of account end, ie, 31 August 2017. As the return is more than three months late, there is a fixed penalty of £200.

        There is also a tax-geared penalty as the return was submitted more than 18 months but less than 24 months after the end of the return period and tax was outstanding at the 18 month point. The penalty is 10% of the unpaid tax.

37 C   £1,000 fixed penalty and no tax-geared penalty

        The return should have been filed within 12 months of the period of account end, ie, 30 April 2017. As the return is more than three months late, there would usually be a £200 fixed penalty. However as this is the third consecutive late return (persistent failure), this is increased to £1,000.

        There is no tax-geared penalty as the return was submitted within 18 months of the end of the return period (31 October 2017). The fact that there was tax unpaid at the 18 month point does not alone give rise to a late filing penalty.

38 C   Blunt Ltd – 31 March 2024

    E   Jim – 31 January 2024

        A company must keep its records for six years from the end of the accounting period. An individual must keep his business records for five years from 31 January following the tax year.

        This question is from the sample paper issued by ICAEW.

39 D £0

The failure to register is not deliberate so there is a maximum penalty of 30% of potential lost revenue.

Edmund registers within 12 months of when he should have and pays the tax due at that time. Therefore the penalty may be reduced to zero.

40 C Daniel's full income tax return for 2017/18 received on 4 July 2018 should be submitted to HMRC by 31 October 2018, if Daniel wants HMRC to calculate the tax

E Frank Ltd's P11D's for 2017/18 should be submitted to HMRC by 6 July 2018.

A VAT return must be submitted electronically seven calendar days after the last day of the month following the end of the return period , ie, 7 April 2018.

The partnership income tax return has to be submitted online by the later of 31 January following the tax year or three months from receiving the return – in this case by 3 February 2019.

Eagle Ltd has one year from the end of the period of account to submit its corporation tax return, ie, by 31 December 2018.

41 C £500

The original default led to a surcharge liability notice but no surcharge. The next default would have given rise to a surcharge at 2%. The VAT payment is late for this quarter (due 7 February 2018), and so there is another default with surcharge at 5% (£500).

42 A £0

The default in respect of the late 30 April return would have given rise to a surcharge liability notice with a surcharge period running for 12 months. Therefore, the return for the quarter ended 31 October 2017 is within this period, and a 2% surcharge arise on the late VAT payment, which was due by 7 December 2017. However, as this is under £400 (£100), the surcharge would not be imposed.

43 B £1,080

The maximum penalty for a 'not deliberate' failure to notify is 30% of potential lost revenue of £10,800.

As HMRC has been notified of the need to register the penalty can be reduced. The tax was unpaid for more than 12 months so the penalty can be reduced to a minimum of 10% of £10,800, ie, £1,080.

44 A Careless

F 0% of potential lost revenue

The error is careless. The disclosure to HMRC is unprompted and therefore the penalty can be reduced to 0% of potential lost revenue.

This question is from the sample paper issued by ICAEW.

45 D A correction cannot be made in the next return because the error exceeds £50,000

The reporting error threshold is the higher of £10,000 and 1% of turnover (£5.6 million @ 1% = £56,000), subject to an overall maximum of £50,000.

The error must therefore be disclosed to HMRC rather than adjusted for in the next return.

46   C   £2,100

Ethel has made a deliberate but not concealed error. The maximum penalty would be 70% of potential lost revenue.

Ethel's prompted disclosure means that the penalty can be reduced to 35% of potential lost revenue.

Potential lost revenue is:

£15,000 × 40% = £6,000

Therefore 35% × £6,000 = £2,100

This question is from the sample paper issued by ICAEW.

47   D   Insufficient funds to pay the tax due

48   D   £46

As this is the third late payment in the tax year the penalty is 1% of the tax unpaid.

49   A   True – A taxpayer may appeal against an information notice

     D   False – A taxpayer has no right of appeal against an inspection notice

50   B   False

     C   True

     F   False

An employer can use voluntary payrolling to report all benefits excluding employer provided living accommodation and beneficial loans.

1

	Marks
Income tax computation	
Interest from loan to Dot and dividends	1
Personal allowance	1
Working 1 – Trading income	
Legal and professional fees	1
Accountancy fees	1
Class 2 NIC	1
VAT re stock purchase	1
Working 2 – Employment income	
Free meals	1
Childcare vouchers	1
Car	2
	10

Mildred's total taxable income for 2017/18

	Non-savings income £	Savings income £	Dividend income £
Trading Income (W1)	32,848		
Employment income (W2)	18,780		
Interest from loan to Dot		100	
Dividends			18,900
Net income	51,628	100	18,900
Personal allowance	(11,500)		
Taxable income	40,128	100	18,900

Tutorial note:

Be very careful to ensure that you use brackets or a minus sign when inputting numbers which are deductible – eg, an allowance, deduction or an expense. In this case, the personal allowance must be input as '(11,500)' not just '11,500'.

W1 – Trading income

	£
Trading profits	30,700
Legal and professional fees	2,000
Accountancy fees	0
Class 2 NIC	148
VAT re stock purchase	0
Tax-adjusted trading profits	32,848

W2 – Employment income

	£
Salary	15,000
Free meals	0
Childcare vouchers	0
Car	3,780
Total employment income	**18,780**

Childcare vouchers

Childcare vouchers of up to £55 per week are exempt as Mildred was in the scheme prior to 6 April 2011.

Car benefit

130 – 95 = 35g/km

35 ÷ 5 = 7%

Taxable percentage 28% (18% + 7% + 3% diesel)

£18,000 × 28% = £5,040

£5,040 × 9/12 = £3,780

The benefit is time apportioned as the car was available from 1 July 2017. List price is used not price paid for the car.

This question is from the sample paper issued by ICAEW

2

Marking guide		Marks

		Marks
Income tax computation		
ISA interest and dividend income	1	
Personal allowance	1	
Working 1 – Trading income		
Bad debt written off	1	
Parking fines	1	
Entertaining	1	
Donation to charity	1	
Working 2 – Employment income		
Bonus	1	
Mobile phone	1	
Car	2	
		10

Elan's total taxable income for 2017/18

	Non-savings income £	Savings income £	Dividend income £
Trading Income (W1)	44,700		
Employment income (W2)	32,900		
ISA interest – exempt		0	
Dividends			112,000
Net income	**77,600**	**0**	**112,000**
Personal allowance	0		
Taxable income	**77,600**	**0**	**112,000**

W1 – Trading income

	£
Trading profits	44,100
Bad debt written off	0
Parking fine – allowable as incurred by employee	0
Entertaining clients	600
Donation to charity	0
Tax-adjusted trading profits	**44,700**

W2 – Employment income

	£
Salary	21,000
Bonus	1,250
Mobile phone – exempt	0
Car	10,650
Total employment income	**32,900**

Bonus

The bonus is taxed in the year of receipt, not in the year to which it relates.

Car benefit

130 – 95 = 35g/km
35 ÷ 5 = 7%

Taxable percentage 25% (18% + 7%)
£20,000 × 25% = £5,000

Fuel benefit

£22,600 × 25% = £5,650
Total car benefit = £5,000 + £5,650 = £10,650

3

Marking guide

	Marks
Income tax computation	
Bank interest and dividend income	1
Personal allowance	1
Working 1 – Trading income	
Fine	1
Donation	1
Overdraft interest	1
Professional fees	1
Working 2 – Employment income	
Pension advice	1
Bicycle	1
Accommodation	2
	10

Becky's total taxable income for 2017/18

	Non-savings income £	Savings income £	Dividend income £
Trading Income (W1)	18,540		
Employment income (W2)	31,125		
Bank interest		175	
Dividends			7,500
Net income	**49,665**	**175**	**7,500**
Personal allowance	(11,500)		
Taxable income	**38,165**	**175**	**7,500**

W1 – Trading income

	£
Draft adjusted profits	19,000
Fine	0
Donation	0
Overdraft interest	(160)
Professional fees	(300)
Tax-adjusted trading profits	**18,540**

Tutorial note:

Be very careful when you are reading the question to ensure that you know whether the sole trader has taken account of the items listed in arriving at the draft taxable trading profits figure. In this question the four items listed had not been included in the draft taxable trading profits figure. Therefore the fine is disallowed (as incurred by the sole trader, and not an employee), as is the Gift Aid donation, and so they are not deducted. The overdraft interest and the professional fees are allowable expenses and are therefore deducted.

W2 – Employment income

	£
Salary	16,000
Pension advice	0
Bicycle	0
Accommodation	15,125
Total employment income	**31,125**

Pension advice

Provision of a pension advice is exempt if provided to all employees and less than £150 per tax year.

Bicycle

Provision of a bicycle is exempt if provided to all employees.

Accommodation

Benefit = annual value + additional yearly rent = £12,000 + [(£200,000 – £75,000) × 2.5% = £3,125] = £15,125

Marking guide

	Marks
Income tax computation	
Direct Saver interest and ISA dividends	1
Personal allowance	1
Working 1 – Trading income	
Gifts	1
Redecorating	1
Donations	1
Legal fees	1
Working 2 – Employment income	
Gift from client	1
Eye test	1
Van	2
	10

Mandy's total taxable income for 2017/18

	Non-savings income £	Savings income £	Dividend income £
Trading Income (W1)	34,550		
Employment income (W2)	26,920		
Direct Saver interest		120	
Dividends – exempt from ISA			0
Net income	61,470	120	0
Personal allowance	(11,500)		
Taxable income	49,970	120	0

W1 – Trading income

	£
Trading profits	34,000
Gifts	300
Redecorating	0
Donation	250
Legal fees	0
Tax-adjusted trading profits	34,550

W2 – Employment income

	£
Salary	25,000
Gift from client – exempt as worth <£250	0
Eye test – exempt	0
Van	1,920
Total employment income	26,920

Van benefits

Van
£3,230 × 6/12 = £1,615

Fuel
£610 × 6/12 = £305

Total = £1,615 + £305 = £1,920
The benefits are time apportioned as the van was available from 1 October 2017.

5

Marks

Income tax computation
Premium bond winnings and dividends	1
Personal allowance	1

Working 1 – Trading income
Staff party	1
Stock donation	1
Salary	1
Loan write off	1

Working 2 – Employment income
Private medical insurance	1
Parking space	1
Childcare vouchers	2
	10

Jorge's total taxable income for 2017/18

	Non-savings income £	Savings income £	Dividend income £
Trading Income (W1)	109,200		
Employment income (W2)	46,644		
Premium bond winnings – exempt		0	
Dividends			950
Net income	**155,844**	**0**	**950**
Personal allowance (net income > £123,000)	0		
Taxable income	**155,844**	**0**	**950**

W1 – Trading income

	£
Trading profits	112,000
Staff party	(800)
Stock donation – allowable to educational establishment	(2,000)
Salary	0
Loan write off – non-trade bad debts disallowable	0
Tax-adjusted trading profits	**109,200**

W2 – Employment income

	£
Salary	45,000
Private medical insurance	500
Parking space	0
Childcare vouchers (£50 – £28) × 52	1,144
Total employment income	**46,644**

Childcare vouchers

Childcare vouchers of up to £28 per week are exempt as the level of Jorge's basic earnings means he is a 'higher rate' taxpayer for these purposes only, and Jorge first started receiving the vouchers in 2013 at the earliest (ie, after April 2011).

Marking guide

	Marks
Income tax computation	
Bank interest and dividends	1
Personal allowance	1
Working 1 – Trading income	
Car lease	1
Employer's NIC	1
Legal fees	1
Depreciation	1
Working 2 – Employment income	
Health and safety course	1
Assets for private use	2
Cookery classes	1
	10

Sandra's total taxable income for 2017/18

	Non-savings income £	Savings income £	Dividend income £
Trading Income (W1)	28,790		
Employment income (W2)	20,265		
Bank interest		100	
Dividends			540
Net income	**49,055**	**100**	**540**
Personal allowance	(11,500)		
Taxable income	**37,555**	**100**	**540**

W1 – Trading income

	£
Trading profits	28,400
Car lease £1,600 × 15%	240
Employer's NIC	0
Legal fees – renewal of short lease allowed	0
Depreciation	150
Tax-adjusted trading profits	**28,790**

W2 – Employment income

	£
Salary	20,000
Health and safety course – exempt work-related training	0
Assets for private use	165
Cookery classes – marginal cost	100
Total employment income	**20,265**

Assets for private use

The provision of the mobile phone is exempt.

TV £825 × 20% = £165

Marking guide

Income tax computation

	Marks
Investment account interest and dividends	1
Personal allowance	1

Working 1 – Trading income

Building work	1
Interest	1
Accountancy fees	1
VAT re advertising	1

Working 2 – Employment income

Pension contribution	1
Car	2
Medical	1
	10

Leanne's total taxable income for 2017/18

	Non-savings income £	Savings income £	Dividend income £
Trading Income (W1)	18,670		
Employment income (W2)	20,340		
Investment account		60	
Dividends			500
Net income	**39,010**	**60**	**500**
Personal allowance	(11,500)		
Taxable income	**27,510**	**60**	**500**

W1 – Trading income

	£
Trading profits	19,500
Building work (capital)	0
Interest (business purpose)	(230)
Accountancy fees	(500)
VAT re advertising – deductible as advertising deductible	(100)
Tax-adjusted trading profits	**18,670**

W2 – Employment income

	£
Salary	18,500
Pension contribution	0
Car	1,840
Medical – one per year exempt	0
Total employment income	**20,340**

Car benefit

Taxable percentage 16% (13% + 3% diesel)
£23,000 × 16% = £3,680
£3,680 × 6/12 = £1,840

The benefit is time apportioned as the car was available from 1 October 2017. List price is used not price paid for the car.

Marking guide

	Marks
Income tax computation	
Repayment interest and dividends	1
Personal allowance	1
Working 1 – Trading income	
Decorating	1
Fine	1
Pension contribution	1
Overdraft fee	1
Working 2 – Employment income	
Bonus	1
Vouchers	1
Camera	2
	10

Simon's total taxable income for 2017/18

	Non-savings income £	Savings income £	Dividend income £
Trading Income (W1)	33,100		
Employment income (W2)	11,285		
Repayment interest – exempt		0	
Dividends			1,000
Net income	**44,385**	**0**	**1,000**
Personal allowance	(11,500)		
Taxable income	**32,885**	**0**	**1,000**

W1 – Trading income

	£
Trading profits	29,600
Decorating	0
Fine	2,000
Pension contribution – appropriation	1,500
Overdraft fee	0
Tax-adjusted trading profits	**33,100**

W2 – Employment income

	£
Salary	10,000
Bonus	200
Vouchers	950
Camera	135
Total employment income	**11,285**

Vouchers

The benefit is the cost to the employer not the face value of the voucher.

Camera

£1,500 × 20% × 9/12 = £225
Benefit = £225 – £90 (employee contribution) = £135.

The benefit is time apportioned as the camera was available from 1 July 2017.

Marking guide

	Marks
Income tax computation	
Treasury stock interest and dividends	1
Personal allowance	1
Working 1 – Trading income	
Pension contribution	1
Patent	1
Diaries	1
Subscription	1
Working 2 – Employment income	
Meal vouchers	1
Accommodation	2
Summer party	1
	10

Finlay's total taxable income for 2017/18

	Non-savings income £	Savings income £	Dividend income £
Trading Income (W1)	45,010		
Employment income (W2)	18,910		
Treasury stock interest		300	
Dividends – exempt			0
Net income	63,920	300	0
Personal allowance	(11,500)		
Taxable income	52,420	300	0

W1 – Trading income

	£
Trading profits	50,000
Pension contribution	(2,100)
Patent	(1,700)
Diaries	(1,000)
Subscription	(190)
Tax-adjusted trading profits	**45,010**

W2 – Employment income

	£
Salary	15,000
Meal vouchers	960
Accommodation	2,950
Summer party	0
Total employment income	**18,910**

Meal vouchers – Benefit = £4 × 240 = £960

Living accommodation

Benefit = £13,000 (higher of rental value and annual value) × 3/12 – £300 (employee contribution) = £2,950

The benefit is time apportioned as the flat was available from 1 January 2018.

Summer party – As the cost in relation to Finlay does not exceed £150 in the tax year, this is an exempt benefit.

Marking guide

	Marks
Income tax computation	
Lottery winnings and dividends	1
Personal allowance	1
Working 1 – Trading income	
Donation	1
Repairs	1
Legal fees	1
Goods	1
Working 2 – Employment income	
Football match	1
Childcare	1
Car	2
	10

Victoria's total taxable income for 2017/18

	Non-savings income £	Savings income £	Dividend income £
Trading Income (W1)	22,700		
Employment income (W2)	129,385		
Lottery winnings – exempt		0	
Dividends			5,000
Net income	**152,085**	**0**	**5,000**
Personal allowance (net income > £123,000)	0		
Taxable income	**152,085**	**0**	**5,000**

W1 – Trading income

	£
Trading profits	19,000
Donation	1,000
Repairs	0
Legal fees	1,500
Goods – selling price must be taxed	1,200
Tax adjusted trading profits	**22,700**

W2 – Employment income

	£
Salary	123,400
Football match – exempt as provided by third party	0
Childcare – exempt as run by her employer	0
Car	5,985
Total employment income	**129,385**

Car benefit

100 – 95 = 5g/km
5 ÷ 5 = 1%

Taxable percentage 19% (18% + 1%)
(£35,000 + £500 – £4,000) × 19% = £5,985

The benefit is calculated on the list price less the employee's contribution of £4,000, plus accessories costing more than £100 added later.

Principles of Taxation: Question Bank

Scenario-based questions: corporation tax

1

		Marks
Kennedy Ltd's Taxable Total Profits		
Non-trading loans		1
Dividends		1
Qualifying donation		1
Working 1 – Trading income		
Depreciation		½
Loan interest payable		½
Qualifying donation		1
Exempt dividends received		½
Bank interest receivable		½
Car leasing charges		1
Capital allowances		1
Corporation tax payment date		
Exempt ABGH distributions		1
Due date		1
		10

(a) **Kennedy Ltd's Taxable Total Profits**

	£
Trading Income (W1)	1,669,830
Non-trading loans (£3,000 – £1,000)	2,000
Dividends	0
Qualifying donation	(3,800)
Taxable total profits	**1,668,030**

W1 – Trading income

	£
Draft accounting profits	1,595,000
Depreciation	202,400
Loan interest payable	1,000
Qualifying donation	6,000
Exempt dividends received	(18,000)
Bank interest receivable	(3,000)
Car leasing charges	(3,570)
Capital allowances (AIA)	(110,000)
Trading income	**1,669,830**

(b) **Corporation tax payment date**

	£
Taxable total profits	1,490,000
Exempt ABGH distributions	25,000
Augmented profits	**1,515,000**

Corporation tax due date for Y/E 31/12/18 is **14/07/2018**

This question is from the sample paper issued by ICAEW.

Marking guide

	Marks
Sigil Ltd's Taxable Total Profits	
Non-trading loans	1
Dividends	1
Chargeable gain	1
Working 1 – Trading income	
Depreciation	½
Loan interest payable	½
Profit on disposal	1
Exempt dividends received	½
Bank interest receivable	½
Employee loan interest	1
Capital allowances	1
Corporation tax payment date	
Exempt ABGH distributions	1
Due date	1
	10

(a) **Sigil Ltd's Taxable Total Profits**

	£
Trading Income (W1)	108,100
Non-trading loans (£800 + £5,000 – £2,000)	3,800
Dividends	0
Chargeable gain	9,000
Taxable total profits	**120,900**

> **Tutorial note:**
>
> Remember that if an item of income is not taxable then you must input a zero into the relevant box to be awarded the mark available.

W1 – Trading income

	£
Draft accounting profits	125,000
Depreciation	6,300
Loan interest payable	2,000
Profit on disposal	(12,000)
Exempt dividends received	(4,000)
Bank interest receivable	(5,000)
Employee loan interest	(600)
Capital allowances (WDA @ 18%)	(3,600)
Trading income	**108,100**

(b) **Corporation tax payment date**

	£
Taxable total profits	213,000
Exempt ABGH distributions	4,000
Augmented profits	**217,000**

Corporation tax due date for Y/E 31/03/19 is **01/01/2020**

3

Marks

Bryn Ltd's Taxable Total Profits

Non-trading loans	1
Dividends	1
Qualifying donation	1

Working 1 – Trading income

Depreciation	½
Loan interest payable	½
Qualifying donation	1
Exempt dividends received	½
Bank interest receivable	½
Gifts	1
Capital allowances	1

Corporation tax payment date

Exempt ABGH distributions	1
Due date	1
	10

(a) **Bryn Ltd's Taxable Total Profits**

	£
Trading Income (W1)	882,000
Non-trading loans	4,200
Dividends	0
Qualifying donation	(1,600)
Taxable total profits	**884,600**

W1 – Trading income

	£
Draft accounting profits	890,000
Depreciation	45,500
Loan interest payable	0
Qualifying donation	8,000
Exempt dividends received	(27,000)
Bank interest receivable	(4,200)
Gifts – £10 × 30	(300)
Capital allowances (FYA)	(30,000)
Trading income	**882,000**

Tutorial note:

Remember that if no adjustment is required then you must input a zero into the relevant box to be awarded the mark available.

(b) **Corporation tax payment date**

	£
Taxable total profits	980,900
Exempt ABGH distributions	50,000
Augmented profits	**1,030,900**

Corporation tax due date for Y/E 30/09/18 is **14/04/2018**

Bryn Ltd has one related 51% group company at the end of the previous accounting period and its augmented profits exceed the limit of £750,000 so the company is large. It was also large in the previous accounting period and so quarterly instalment payments are required.

Marking guide

	Marks
Lundy Ltd's Taxable Total Profits	
Non-trading loans	1
Dividends	1
Property income	1
Working 1 – Trading income	
Depreciation	½
Loan interest payable	½
Property income	1
Exempt dividends received	½
Bank interest receivable	½
Legal fees	1
Capital allowances	1
Corporation tax payment date	
Exempt ABGH distributions	1
Due date	1
	10

(a) **Lundy Ltd's Taxable Total Profits**

	£
Trading Income (W1)	2,964,000
Non-trading loans (£7,000 – £3,800)	3,200
Dividends	0
Property income	30,000
Taxable total profits	**2,997,200**

W1 – Trading income

	£
Draft accounting profits	2,860,000
Depreciation	148,700
Loan interest payable	3,800
Property income	(25,000)
Exempt dividends received	(9,000)
Bank interest receivable	(7,000)
Legal fees	(300)
Capital allowances (WDA @ 18%)	(7,200)
Trading income	**2,964,000**

(b) **Corporation tax payment date**

	£
Taxable total profits	3,100,000
Exempt ABGH distributions	9,000
Augmented profits	**3,109,000**

Corporation tax due date for Y/E 31/03/19 is **14/10/2018**

5

Marks

Knight Ltd's Taxable Total Profits
Non-trading loans	1
Dividends	1
Property income	1

Working 1 – Trading income
Depreciation	½
Loan interest payable	½
Property income	1
Exempt dividends received	½
Bank interest receivable	½
Marketing fees	1
Capital allowances	1

Corporation tax payment date
Exempt ABGH distributions	1
Due date	1
	10

(a) **Knight Ltd's Taxable Total Profits**

	£
Trading Income (W1)	370,700
Non-trading loans	5,100
Dividends	0
Property income (£40,000 × 9/12)	30,000
Taxable total profits	**405,800**

W1 – Trading income

	£
Draft accounting profits	467,000
Depreciation	32,500
Loan interest payable	0
Property income	(40,000)
Exempt dividends received	(4,500)
Bank interest receivable	(5,100)
Marketing fees	800
Capital allowances (AIA)	(80,000)
Trading income	**370,700**

(b) **Corporation tax payment date**

	£
Taxable total profits	420,000
Exempt ABGH distributions	0
Augmented profits	**420,000**

Corporation tax due date for Y/E 31/12/18 is **01/10/2019**

Even with one related 51% group company at the end of the previous accounting period, Knight Ltd's augmented profits do not exceed the limit (£750,000) and so quarterly instalment payments are not required.

The dividends from Sword Ltd are not included in augmented profits as they are received from a 51% subsidiary.

Marking guide

	Marks
Budding Ltd's Taxable Total Profits	
Non-trading loans	1
Dividends	1
Qualifying donation	1
Working 1 – Trading income	
Depreciation	½
Bonuses	½
Qualifying donation	1
Exempt dividends received	½
Bank interest receivable	½
Legal fees	1
Capital allowances	1
Corporation tax payment date	
Profits limit	1
Due date	1
	10

(a) **Budding Ltd's Taxable Total Profits**

	£
Trading Income (W1)	195,850
Non-trading loans	8,000
Dividends	0
Qualifying donation	(8,300)
Taxable total profits	**195,550**

W1 – Trading income

	£
Draft accounting profits	165,000
Depreciation	13,200
Bonuses	25,000
Qualifying donation	10,000
Exempt dividends received	(6,750)
Bank interest receivable	(8,000)
Legal fees	(1,800)
Capital allowances (small pool write off)	(800)
Trading income	**195,850**

(b) **Corporation tax limit and payment date**

The profits limit is | 1,000,000

Corporation tax due date | 01/09/2019

Marking guide

	Marks
Pedestal Ltd's Taxable Total Profits	
Non-trading loans	1
Qualifying donation	1
Working 1 – Trading income	
Depreciation	½
HMRC interest payable	½
Donation	1
Client entertaining	½
Bank interest receivable	½
Loan stock	1
Capital allowances	2
Corporation tax payment date	
Exempt ABGH distributions	1
Due date	1
	10

(a) **Pedestal Ltd's Taxable Total Profits**

	£
Trading Income (W1)	1,898,550
Non-trading loans (£7,200 – £150)	7,050
Qualifying donation	(8,000)
Taxable total profits	**1,897,600**

W1 – Trading income

	£
Draft accounting profits	1,873,000
Depreciation	80,900
HMRC interest payable	150
Donation	10,000
Client entertaining	6,300
Bank interest receivable	(7,200)
Loan stock	(3,800)
Capital allowances (AIA)	(60,800)
Trading income	**1,898,550**

The capital allowances are calculated as the machinery which is eligible for the AIA (max amount = £200,000 × 6/12 as accounting period is only six months), plus the normal WDA @ 18% x 6/12 on the TWDV b/fwd:

£50,000 + (£120,000 × 18% × 6/12) = £60,800

As the loan stock was issued for trading purposes, both the interest and legal fees are trading expenses.

(b) **Corporation tax payment date**

	£
Taxable total profits	1,940,000
Exempt ABGH distributions	7,000
Augmented profits	**1,947,000**

Corporation tax due date for Y/E 31/12/18 is **14/07/2018**

Marking guide

	Marks
Mayet Ltd's Taxable Total Profits	
Non-trading loans	1
Dividends	1
Qualifying donation	1
Working 1 – Trading income	
Depreciation	½
Pension cost	½
Qualifying donation	1
Exempt dividends received	½
Bank interest receivable	½
Debt write-offs	1
Capital allowances	1
Corporation tax payment date	
Exempt ABGH distributions	1
Due date	1
	10

(a) **Mayet Ltd's Taxable Total Profits**

	£
Trading Income (W1)	71,500
Non-trading loans	13,000
Dividends	0
Qualifying donation	(16,000)
Taxable total profits	68,500

W1 – Trading income

	£
Draft accounting profits	95,000
Depreciation	4,500
Pension cost	2,000
Qualifying donation	14,000
Exempt dividends received	(11,700)
Bank interest receivable	(13,000)
Debt write-offs	(7,000)
Capital allowances (FYA)	(12,300)
Trading income	71,500

(b) **Corporation tax payment date**

	£
Taxable total profits	100,000
Exempt ABGH distributions	12,000
Augmented profits	112,000

Corporation tax due date for Y/E 30/06/18 is **01/04/2019**

Marking guide

	Marks
Fonic Ltd's Taxable Total Profits	
Non-trading loans	1
Dividends	1
Property income	1
Working 1 – Trading income	
Depreciation	½
Profit on disposal	½
Property income	1
Exempt dividends received	½
Bank interest receivable	½
Entertaining	1
Capital allowances	1
Corporation tax payment date	
Limit	1
Due date	1
	10

(a) **Fonic Ltd's Taxable Total Profits**

	£
Trading Income (W1)	955,900
Non-trading loans	4,900
Dividends	0
Property income	18,000
Taxable total profits	**978,800**

W1 – Trading income

	£
Draft accounting profits	852,000
Depreciation	130,600
Profit on disposal	(2,000)
Property income	(16,500)
Exempt dividends received	(10,800)
Bank interest receivable	(4,900)
Entertaining	4,000
Capital allowances (balancing charge)	3,500
Trading income	**955,900**

(b) **Corporation tax limit and payment date**

The profits limit is	750,000

Corporation tax due date	01/07/2019

Marking guide

		Marks
Selby Ltd's Taxable Total Profits		
Non-trading loans	1	
Qualifying donation	1	
Working 1 – Trading income		
Depreciation	½	
Loan interest payable	½	
Qualifying donation	1	
Pension contributions	½	
Bank interest receivable	½	
Professional fees	1	
Capital allowances	2	
Corporation tax payment date		
Exempt ABGH distributions	1	
Due date	1	
		10

(a) **Selby Ltd's Taxable Total Profits**

	£
Trading Income (W1)	408,520
Non-trading loans	6,000
Qualifying donation	(1,800)
Taxable total profits	**412,720**

W1 – Trading income

	£
Draft accounting profits	534,000
Depreciation	46,200
Loan interest payable	0
Qualifying donation	2,000
Pension contributions	22,000
Bank interest receivable	(6,000)
Professional fees	(580)
Capital allowances	(189,100)
Trading income	**408,520**

The capital allowances are calculated as the purchase price of the machinery which is eligible for the AIA, plus the normal WDA @ 18% on the TWDV bf:

£175,600 + (£75,000 × 18%) = £189,100

(b) **Corporation tax payment date**

	£
Taxable total profits	480,000
Exempt ABGH distributions	0
Augmented profits	**480,000**

Corporation tax due date for Y/E 31/12/18 is **01/10/2019**

Even with a related 51% group company, Selby Ltd's augmented profits do not exceed the limit (£750,000) and so quarterly instalment payments are not required.

PRINCIPLES OF TAXATION

Tax Tables Finance Act 2017

The tax tables reproduced on the following pages are identical to the tax tables you will be given in the exam. Familiarise yourself with the content so that you know what you need to learn and what you can access in the exam from the tax tables.

In the actual exam, for ease of use on screen, your tax tables are divided into sections in accordance with the five key syllabus areas. You will find that for each question in the actual exam you will only be able to access the part of the tax tables relevant to that part of the syllabus. This is to minimise the amount of time you will need to spend scrolling through the tax tables.

Questions on each syllabus area will therefore only be able to access the pages of the tax tables as follows:

- Administration   pages 181-185
- Income tax & NIC   pages 186-187
- Capital gains   page 188
- Corporation tax   page 189
- VAT   page 190

ICAEW – CERTIFICATE LEVEL

TAX TABLES FA2017

SYLLABUS AREA: ADMINISTRATION

SUBMISSION DATES

Submission dates for 2017/18 personal self-assessment tax returns

Return filed online	Later of: • 31 January 2019 • 3 months from the date of issue of return
Paper returns[1]	Later of: • 31 October 2018 • 3 months from the date of issue of return

(1)   If HMRC is to calculate tax due on a paper return, the filing date is the later of 31 October 2018 and two months from the date the notice to make a return was issued.

Submission dates for corporation tax returns

Must be filed by 12 months from the end of the period of account.

Submission dates for PAYE information: Real Time Information

Information	Filing date
Full Payment Submission (FPS)	On or before the day the employee is paid
P60 (to employees)	31 May following the tax year end
P11D	6 July following the tax year end

PAYMENT DATES

Payment dates for income tax

Payment	Filing date
First interim payment [1]	31 January in the tax year
Second interim payment [1]	31 July following the tax year end
Balancing payment	31 January following the tax year end

(1)   Interim payments are not required if the tax paid by assessment for the previous year was less than:
   • £1,000; or
   • 20% of the total tax liability (income tax and Class 4).

Payment dates for capital gains tax

Capital gains tax is payable by 31 January following the tax year end.

Payment dates for corporation tax

Corporation tax	Nine months and one day after the end of an accounting period
Corporation tax by instalments	The 14th day of months 7, 10, 13 and 16 counted from the start of a 12-month accounting period

Payment dates for VAT

	Due date
Electronic payment	7 calendar days after the last day of the month following the end of the return period
Direct debit payment	Collected automatically 3 working days after electronic payment due date

ICAEW - CERTIFICATE LEVEL
TAX TABLES FA2017

SYLLABUS AREA: ADMINISTRATION

MAIN PENALTY PROVISIONS

RECORD KEEPING PENALTY

Offence	Maximum Penalty
Failure to keep and retain tax records	£3,000 per tax year / accounting period

INDIVIDUALS: PENALTIES

Offence	Maximum Penalty
Failure to notify chargeability by 5 October following tax year end	See below: penalties for failure to notify
Late payment of income tax or capital gains tax: [1] • Unpaid 30 days after payment due date • Unpaid 6 months after payment due date • Unpaid 12 months after payment due date	 5% of tax unpaid Further 5% of tax unpaid Further 5% of tax unpaid

(1)   Late payment penalties do not apply to payments on account.

Income tax and CGT: penalties for late filing of a self-assessment return

Offence	Maximum Penalty
Late return	Immediate £100 fixed penalty
Return more than 3 months late	Daily fixed penalties of up to £10 per day for maximum 90 days
Return more than 6 months but less than 12 months late	Further tax geared penalty of 5% of tax due (minimum £300)
Return 12 months late	Further tax geared penalties apply (minimum £300): • 100% if deliberate and concealed[1] • 70% if deliberate but not concealed[1] • 5% in all other cases

(1)   These tax geared penalties are reduced for disclosure as per penalties for incorrect returns.

COMPANIES: PENALTIES

Offence	Maximum Penalty
Failure to notify chargeability within 12 months of end of accounting period	See below: penalties for failure to notify

Corporation tax: penalties for late filing of a corporation tax return

Offence	Penalty[1]
Late return, up to 3 months late	£100 fixed penalty, or £500 for persistent failure
Return more than 3 months late	£200 fixed penalty, or £1,000 for persistent failure
Return filed more than 18 months but less than 24 months after end of return period	Tax geared penalty of 10% of tax unpaid 18 months after end of return period
Return filed more than 24 months after end of return period	Tax geared penalty of 20% of tax unpaid 18 months after end of return period

(1)   The tax geared penalty is charged in addition to the fixed penalty but only one of each type of penalty is charged.

SYLLABUS AREA: ADMINISTRATION

PAYE: penalties for late returns/ submissions

Number of employees	Monthly penalty
1 to 9	£100
10 to 49	£200
50 to 249	£300
250 or more	£400

If the form is more than three months late, an additional penalty is due of 5% of the tax and NIC that should have been reported.

Additionally, there is a £300 penalty per late P11D return, with an extra £60 per day charged if the delay continues.

PAYE: penalties for late payment

	No of late payments	% of tax unpaid[1]
Penalties for late payment of in-year PAYE depend on the number of defaults in the tax year	1st	nil
	2nd, 3rd & 4th	1%
	5th, 6th & 7th	2%
	8th, 9th & 10th	3%
	11th or more	4%
Where a penalty has been imposed and the tax remains unpaid at 6 months		5%[2]
Where a penalty has been imposed and the tax remains unpaid at 12 months		5%[2]

(1)   The percentage penalty is applied to the total amount that is late in the relevant tax month.

(2)   The 6 month and the possible further 12 month penalties are in addition to the initial penalty for late payment.

VAT: penalties

Offence	Maximum Penalty
Failure to notify liability for registration or change in nature of supplies by person exempted from registration	See below: penalties for failure to notify

VAT: late payment or late filing – default surcharge

Default involving late payment of VAT in the surcharge period[1]	Surcharge as a percentage of the VAT outstanding at the due date
First	2%[2]
Second	5%[2]
Third	10%[3]
Fourth	15%[3]

(1)   Default if late payment of VAT or filing of VAT return and surcharge liability notice issued, but default surcharge only on late payment.

(2)   No surcharge if would be less than £400.

(3)   Minimum £30 payable.

VAT errors

An error made on a VAT return can be corrected on the next return provided it was not deliberate and does not exceed the greater of:

* £10,000 (net under-declaration minus over-declaration); or
* 1% × net VAT turnover for return period (maximum £50,000)

Alternatively, a 'small' error which is not deliberate may be corrected via the submission of form VAT652. Errors which are not 'small' or errors which are deliberate should be notified to HMRC on form VAT652.

ICAEW - CERTIFICATE LEVEL

TAX TABLES FA2017

SYLLABUS AREA: ADMINISTRATION

PENALTIES FOR INCORRECT RETURNS

The penalties are a percentage of the potential lost revenue

Reason for penalty	Maximum penalty	Minimum penalty with unprompted disclosure	Minimum penalty with prompted disclosure
Careless action	30%	Nil	15%
Deliberate but not concealed action	70%	20%	35%
Deliberate and concealed action	100%	30%	50%

PENALTIES FOR FAILURE TO NOTIFY

Failures to notify chargeability to tax, or liability to register for tax that leads to a loss of tax will result in a penalty. The penalties are a percentage of the potential lost revenue.

Reason for penalty	Maximum penalty	Minimum penalty with unprompted disclosure		Minimum penalty with prompted disclosure	
Deliberate and concealed action	100%	30%		50%	
Deliberate but not concealed action	70%	20%		35%	
		>12m	<12m	>12m	<12m
Any other case	30%	10%	Nil	20%	10%

INCOME TAX RATES: 2017/18	Rate	Taxable income band
Main rates		
Basic rate	20%	£1 – £33,500
Higher rate	40%	£33,501 – £150,000
Additional rate	45%	Over £150,000
Savings rates		
Starting rate for savings	0%	£1 - £5,000
Savings income nil rate	0%	First £1,000 or £500
Savings basic rate	20%	Up to £33,500
Savings higher rate	40%	Up to £150,000
Savings additional rate	45%	Over £150,000
Dividends rates		
Dividend nil rate	0%	£5,000
Dividend ordinary rate	7.5%	Otherwise chargeable at basic rate
Dividend upper rate	32.5%	Otherwise chargeable at higher rate
Dividend additional rate	38.1%	Otherwise chargeable at additional rate
Default rates		
Default basic rate	20%	
Default higher rate	40%	
Default additional rate	45%	

INCOME TAX RELIEFS	2017/18
Personal allowance	£11,500

ICAEW – CERTIFICATE LEVEL
TAX TABLES FA2017

SYLLABUS AREA: ADMINISTRATION

CGT RATES	2017/18
Gains falling within the remaining basic rate band	10%
Gains exceeding the basic rate band	20%

CORPORATION TAX RATES	FY 2017
Tax rate	19%
Augmented profits limit for corporation tax payment dates	£1,500,000

NATIONAL INSURANCE CONTRIBUTIONS

NIC CLASS 1 CONTRIBUTIONS	2017/18		
	Annual	Monthly	Weekly
Primary threshold (PT)	£8,164	£680	£157
Secondary threshold (ST)	£8,164	£680	£157
Upper earnings limit (UEL)	£45,000	£3,750	£866
Apprentice upper secondary threshold (AUST) for under 25s	£45,000	£3,750	£866
Upper secondary threshold (UST) for under 21s	£45,000	£3,750	£866

Employment allowance (per year, per employer)	£3,000
Class 1 Primary contributions on earnings between PT & UEL	12%
Class 1 Primary contributions on earnings above UEL	2%
Class 1 Secondary contributions on earnings above ST where employee aged 21 or over and not an apprentice under the age of 25	13.8%
Class 1 Secondary contributions on earnings between ST & AUST for apprentices under the age of 25	0%
Class 1 Secondary contributions on earnings above AUST for apprentices under the age of 25	13.8%
Class 1 Secondary contributions on earnings between ST & UST for employees under the age of 21	0%
Class 1 Secondary contributions on earnings above UST for employees under the age of 21	13.8%
Class 1A contributions	13.8%

NIC CLASS 2 CONTRIBUTIONS	2017/18
Normal rate	£2.85 pw
Small profits threshold	£6,025 pa

NIC CLASS 4 CONTRIBUTIONS	
Annual lower profits limit (LPL)	£8,164
Annual upper profits limit (UPL)	£45,000
Percentage rate between LPL & UPL	9%
Percentage rate above UPL	2%

VAT	
Standard rate of VAT	20%
Reduced rate of VAT	5%

SYLLABUS AREA: INCOME TAX & NIC

INCOME TAX RATES: 2017/18	Rate	Taxable income band
Main rates		
Basic rate	20%	£1 – £33,500
Higher rate	40%	£33,501 – £150,000
Additional rate	45%	Over £150,000
Savings rates		
Starting rate for savings	0%	£1 - £5,000
Savings income nil rate	0%	First £1,000 or £500
Savings basic rate	20%	Up to £33,500
Savings higher rate	40%	Up to £150,000
Savings additional rate	45%	Over £150,000
Dividends rates		
Dividend nil rate	0%	£5,000
Dividend ordinary rate	7.5%	Otherwise chargeable at basic rate
Dividend upper rate	32.5%	Otherwise chargeable at higher rate
Dividend additional rate	38.1%	Otherwise chargeable at additional rate
Default rates		
Default basic rate	20%	
Default higher rate	40%	
Default additional rate	45%	

INCOME TAX RELIEFS	2017/18
Personal allowance[1]	£11,500
Marriage allowance where both born after 5 April 1935[2]	
– Marriage allowance	£1,150
Married couple's allowance (relief is given at 10%)	
– At least one spouse/partner born before 6 April 1935	£8,445
– Maximum income before abatement of relief[3]	£28,000
– Minimum allowance	£3,260

(1) The personal allowance of any individual with adjusted net income above £100,000 is reduced by £1 for every £2 of adjusted net income above the £100,000 limit.

(2) A spouse or civil partner who is a basic rate taxpayer or who has income of less than the personal allowance is allowed to transfer £1,150 (ie 10%) of their personal allowance to their spouse/civil partner provided the recipient spouse is a basic rate taxpayer.

(3) This is the income limit for abatement of the married couple's allowance by £1 for every £2 over the limit.

COMPANY CARS, VANS AND FUEL

Company cars

Cash equivalent   9% of list price for cars emitting 0–50g/km
13% of list price for cars emitting 51–75g/km
17% of list price for cars emitting 76–94g/km
18% of list price for cars emitting 95–99g/km
Increased by 1% per 5g/km over the 95g/km relevant threshold
Capped at 37% of list price
3% supplement on all diesel cars (subject to 37% cap)

Private fuel provided for company car

£22,600 × company car %

SYLLABUS AREA: INCOME TAX & NIC

Van scale charge

£3,230 if van has CO_2 emissions and £646 if it has zero CO_2 emissions

Additional £610 if private fuel provided for the van

Neither charge applies if there is insignificant private use

CAPITAL ALLOWANCES

First year allowances available

100% on new and unused zero emissions goods vehicles
100% on new energy saving plant or machinery
100% on new and unused low emission cars ie, electrically propelled or with CO_2 emissions of not more than 75 g/km (95g/km before 1 April 2015)

Annual investment allowance

£200,000 pa of expenditure incurred by any business on certain plant and machinery from 1 January 2016.

Writing down allowances

18% pa in the main pool

NATIONAL INSURANCE CONTRIBUTIONS

NIC CLASS 1 CONTRIBUTIONS	2017/18 Annual	Monthly	Weekly
Primary threshold (PT)	£8,164	£680	£157
Secondary threshold (ST)	£8,164	£680	£157
Upper earnings limit (UEL)	£45,000	£3,750	£866
Apprentice upper secondary threshold (AUST) for under 25s	£45,000	£3,750	£866
Upper secondary threshold (UST) for under 21s	£45,000	£3,750	£866

Employment allowance (per year, per employer)	£3,000
Class 1 Primary contributions on earnings between PT & UEL	12%
Class 1 Primary contributions on earnings above UEL	2%
Class 1 Secondary contributions on earnings above ST where employee aged 21 or over and not an apprentice under the age of 25	13.8%
Class 1 Secondary contributions on earnings between ST & AUST for apprentices under the age of 25	0%
Class 1 Secondary contributions on earnings above AUST for apprentices under the age of 25	13.8%
Class 1 Secondary contributions on earnings between ST & UST for employees under the age of 21	0%
Class 1 Secondary contributions on earnings above UST for employees under the age of 21	13.8%
Class 1A contributions	13.8%

NIC CLASS 2 CONTRIBUTIONS	2017/18
Normal rate	£2.85 pw
Small profits threshold	£6,025 pa

NIC CLASS 4 CONTRIBUTIONS	
Annual lower profits limit (LPL)	£8,164
Annual upper profits limit (UPL)	£45,000
Percentage rate between LPL & UPL	9%
Percentage rate above UPL	2%

ICAEW - CERTIFICATE LEVEL
TAX TABLES FA2017

SYLLABUS AREA: INCOME TAX & NIC

PAYE CODES

L   tax code with personal allowance

M   tax code with personal allowance plus claiming marriage allowance

N   tax code with personal allowance less surrendered marriage allowance

K   total allowances are less than total deductions

T   tax code includes other calculations to work the personal allowance, for example it has been reduced because estimated annual income is more than £100,000

SYLLABUS AREA: CAPITAL GAINS

	2017/18
Annual exempt amount	£11,300
Gains falling within the remaining basic rate band	10%
Gains exceeding the basic rate band	20%
Basic rate band	£1 – £33,500

ICAEW - CERTIFICATE LEVEL
TAX TABLES FA2017

SYLLABUS AREA: CORPORATION TAX

Financial year	FY 2017
Tax rate	19%
Augmented profits limit for corporation tax payment dates	£1,500,000

CAPITAL ALLOWANCES

First year allowances available

100% on new and unused zero emissions goods vehicles
100% on new energy saving plant or machinery
100% on new and unused low emission cars ie, electrically propelled or with CO_2 emissions of not more than 75 g/km (95g/km before 1 April 2015)

Annual investment allowance

£200,000 pa of expenditure incurred by any company on certain plant and machinery from 1 January 2016.

Writing down allowances

18% pa in the main pool

SYLLABUS AREA: VALUE ADDED TAX

Standard rate		20%
Reduced rate		5%
Annual registration limit	From 1 April 2017	£85,000
De-registration limit	From 1 April 2017	£83,000
VAT fraction (standard rated)		1/6

Cash accounting	**£**
Turnover threshold to join scheme	1,350,000
Turnover threshold to leave scheme	1,600,000

Annual accounting	
Turnover threshold to join scheme	1,350,000
Turnover threshold to leave scheme	1,600,000

Flat rate scheme	
Annual taxable turnover limit (excluding VAT) to join scheme	150,000
Annual total income (including VAT) to leave scheme	230,000

Mock exam
guidance notes

Exam standard

The mock exam should be set at the level of difficulty represented by the 2016 sample paper on the ICAEW website.

Exam format

20% of the marks are allocated from two scenario-based questions. These will each cover a single syllabus area. The remaining 80% of the marks are from 40 objective test questions.

Style of exam questions

The scenario-based questions will each cover a single syllabus area: income tax and NIC, and corporation tax

Each objective test question should conform to the style used in the sample paper ie:

- Multiple Choice Questions (MCQ) (1 from 4 or 5), **or**

- Multi-Part Multiple Choice Questions (MPMCQ), **or**

- Multiple Response Questions (MRQ) (2 from 4 or 5, or possibly 3 from 5), **or**

- 2 MCQ (eg, 2 × 'adjust or do not adjust', or 2 × 'chargeable gain, allowable loss, nil'), **or**

- 3 MCQ (eg, 3 × 'income tax or corporation tax, income tax or capital gains tax, corporation tax or capital gains tax') **or**

- Numerical entry.

Also, there should be no more than 5–6 questions which require either simple yes/no or true/false answers. The mock exam should include two numerical entry questions in total, from syllabus section 6e.

Exam coverage and balance

A mock exam should reflect the weightings in the syllabus specification grid as follows:

Syllabus Area	Weighting	Number of Qs
Objectives, types of tax and ethics	10%	5
Administration of taxation	20%	10
Income tax and national insurance contributions	26%	8 objective test and 1 scenario-based
Capital gains tax and chargeable gains for companies	10%	5
Corporation tax	14%	2 objective test and 1 scenario-based
VAT	20%	10
Total	**100%**	**40 objective test and 2 scenario-based**

A good mock might contain the following balance of questions:

Question No	Syllabus reference	Example
–	3a, 3c, 3e, 3j	Income tax scenario-based question
–	5b, 5c, 5d	Corporation tax scenario-based question
1	1b	Objectives of tax
2	1e	Liability to different taxes
3	1g	Ethics – threats
4	1h	Ethics – money laundering
5	1h	Ethics – tax avoidance v tax evasion
6	2a	Records
7	2b	Calculate a PAYE tax code
8	2c	Self-assessment
9	2d	Due dates
10	2d	Due dates
11	2e	Interest and penalties
12	2e	Interest and penalties
13	2e	Interest and penalties
14	2e	Interest and penalties
15	2f	Enquiries
16	3b	Calculate a personal allowance
17	3d	Badges of trade
18	3e	Calculate capital allowances for sole trader
19	3f	Allocate adjusted profits to partners
20	3g	Opening year rules
21	3i	Closing year rules
22	3j	Calculate income tax liability
23	3k	NIC payable
24	4a	Chargeable & exempt disposals
25	4b	Chattel rules
26	4b	Identify allowable costs for a company
27	4b	Calculate indexed gain for a company
28	4d	Calculate CGT liability
29	5a	Identify correct chargeable accounting periods
30	5d	Identify whether resident in UK
31	6b	Determine total taxable supplies

Question No	Syllabus reference	Example
32	6c	Identify when should register
33	6c	Identify correct rules re registration & deregistration
34	6d	Identify the tax point
35	6e	Recoverability of pre-registration input VAT
36	6e	Calculate recoverable input VAT
37	6e	Calculate output VAT payable
38	6e	VAT and discounts
39	6f	Recognise correct rules for special schemes
40	6f	Calculate VAT due under flat rate scheme